An
English Experience

Exploring the Backroads and Byways
of
Gloucestershire, Wiltshire
and
Hampshire

An English Experience

Exploring the Backroads and Byways
of
Gloucestershire, Wiltshire
and
Hampshire

❧ ❧ ❧

Marge D. Hansen

Published by
Poncha Press
P.O. Box 280
Morrison, CO 80465
SAN: 253-3588
www.ponchapress.com

Printed in Canada
ISBN: 0-9701862-6-6
Library of Congress Pre-assigned Control Number: 2002113294

NOTICE: While every effort has been made by the author and publisher to present accurate information, we cannot be responsible for any injury or loss to persons who refer to or use this book.

To Leona
who often said, "You should write a book."
Thanks for your confidence in me, Mom.
Now I have.

Acknowledgements

Thanks to the many people in England and America whose knowledge, conversations, clever comments and distinctive insights made the writing of this book possible.

Thanks to Rae for keeping us on the right, I mean left, I mean correct side of the road and for sharing the journey.

Thanks to the "flat tire" man who heroically stripped off the old and put on the spare so we could continue on our way.

Thanks to a very special group of women writers for their valuable time and constructive support.

Most importantly, a very special thank you to my family—Richard, Kirsten and Jon—for their patience, understanding, encouragement and ability to listen to another story ... just one more time.

Contents

Hampshire

Less Familiar Words and Terms

Introduction

Britain is kings and queens, magnificent abbeys and peaceful churchyards. It is the story of global influence and, in more recent times, a turning of that tide. But most of all it is the countryside. Rainwashed stone walls border pastoral fields. Daffodils search for the sun as they tumble down hillsides. The dappled bark of ancient trees is reflected in meandering waterways that almost touch the undersides of low footbridges as they cross rushing streams.

The stories on these pages are based on legends as well as historical fact. They tell of people who have lived on this land for centuries: special events in their lives, their accomplishments, why to this day they remain a living part of the country's narrative. There are chapters chronicling familiar sights synonymous with rural Britain: thatched cottages, honey-colored Cotswold stone, sacred yew trees, traditional pubs and the universally recognized English garden. They touch on ancient spirituality and the influence of the Romans.

Each chapter is divided into four sections: the tale, information on the village or town today, finding your way by referencing a large town to help readers identify a map point, and nearby places of interest.

England has its signature attractions and hidden surprises. This companion travel guide is for those who are intrigued by turning off the "big city" tourist trail to discover what the backroads and byways might reveal. These are the simple pleasures that define *An English Experience*.

To the Reader ...

It is often said that taking a trip is a fifty-fifty proposition: Half the fun is the planning; the other half is enjoying the reality of the experience. Learning about the history, culture and customs of the place you plan to visit certainly adds a rewarding dimension to the adventure. Hopefully, reading these chapters will encourage you to add a side trip or two to your English itinerary. Count these places not necessarily as destinations but enhancements to your journey.

One chapter in each section is written in story form, relating the essence of historical characters and customs in a style different from the other chapters. This approach presents names, dates and events in a factual yet somewhat fanciful way. The highly visual presentation of all the material in the book is an effort to capture the reader's attention by painting word pictures that spark the imagination.

Some of the places are well-known. Others are quiet, out-of-the-way spots. All can be reached by exploring the network of roads that wind through the countryside. The directions in each chapter orient drivers to a specific large town or city. Invest in a detailed atlas or ordinance survey map. They reveal major and minor roads that will help you find your way.

"A" roads are main highways, "B" routes are secondary highways, and the smaller roads have no names or numbers to clearly identify them. Signposts guide you, and when they disappear—as they sometimes do—the real fun begins. Driver and navigator work together to decipher the left from the right hand turns, remembering that this is England: Keep the car on the left side of the road!

The backroads offer an unhurried view of the passing landscape. Part of the challenge is to find a place and enjoy the satisfaction of uncovering the seemingly hidden setting. Don't worry about getting lost. It may turn out to be one of the best parts of the trip. Distances are short. Even if you do get turned around, it won't take long to get back on track. And detours often provide unexpected and wonderful discoveries.

Be sure to check opening days and times of any attraction you plan to visit. They can be somewhat irregular and highly seasonal.

The English countryside invites you to put away timetables, explore and spend quiet moments taking pleasure in the beauty of your surroundings. Country lanes, hemmed in by hedgerows, divide and conquer as they converge again on the edge of a small village, twisting into town from different directions. A sense of history and natural beauty make their presence felt here in the grand architecture of a cathedral and the simple, artful furrows of a farmer's field. It's all just waiting for your arrival.

~ M.D.H.

Exploring Glouscestershire, Wiltshire and Hampshire

Great Britain

London

Stanton
Winchcombe
Northleach*
Eastleachs *
Painswick *
Chedworth
GLOUCESTERSHIRE

Lacock
Castle Combe *
Avebury

WILTSHIRE

Stourton
Great Wishford *

Wherwell

Chawton *

Tichborne
Hambledon *

HAMPSHIRE

All locations approximate

Gloucestershire

Chapter One

Stanton

Of
Stones and Sheep

The heart and character of Gloucestershire's Cotswold countryside is easily identified by the charm of its engaging stone villages and the flocks of sheep that amble across the abundant, rolling pastureland. Stately manor houses and magnificent wool churches, so named because profits from wool made their construction possible, were built by merchants who sold the valuable fleeces and shared their largesse with the communities in which they lived.

The buildings of a typical Cotswold village cluster close to one another, presenting a pleasing portrait. Each is just a shade lighter or slightly darker than the one next door. Garden walls offer long, low, mortarless stacks for vines to climb and flowers to peek over. Nature's quarry provides a monochromatic palette unique to each location. The eastern villages are a warm, rich, golden-tan. Moving west, the distinctive honey-colored, buff shades change to a soft, silvery gray.

For centuries, the plentiful oolitic limestone that lies just below the surface of the land has been used in the construction of churches, simple cottages, grand houses, and the walls that separate fields and farms. It was fashioned millions of years ago when skeletons of marine creatures and gritty residue from the sea bed that covered the region combined to make the stone.

Readily excavated, the soft rock is easy to carve and shape but hardens when exposed to the elements. Mullioned windows and decorative moldings adorn houses and shops which grow more beautiful with time and the changing of seasons. Gabled roofs are tiled with thin, small pieces of the stone. They have whimsical names that relate to their individual size: short bachelors, long wibbuts, movities, short elevens, middle becks. The harmonious fusion of textures and colors flecked by patchy traces of moss achieves a handsome effect. Buildings blend with bridges and market crosses. It's as if entire villages materialized in unison and the lush lawns and leafy trees gathered round to make the setting picture-perfect.

Surrounding the villages and towns are the wolds—acres of open, grassy hillsides—which have always supported grazing. Skeletal remains found near Cirencester, known in Roman times as the settlement of Corinium, seem to indicate the Romans introduced a broad-bodied breed of sheep that was most likely the ancestor of the "Cotswold Lion." This sturdy specimen yielded long, wavy, fine wool of excellent quality.

In medieval times, the wool trade brought great wealth to England. Most of the wool was sold abroad to countries that did not have expansive, undeveloped land suitable for constant grazing. Pack horses carried bales of wool from the Cotswolds to the south of England where they were shipped to the Continent.

During the sixteenth and seventeenth centuries, the Cotswold wool industry changed significantly when emphasis was placed on manufacturing material rather than exporting fleece. Many towns and villages along the region's plentiful rivers gave themselves over entirely to the building of waterwheel-powered mills and the production of woven cloth.

Later, when steam engines were introduced to run the machinery, a number of mills shut down. Many villages fell on hard times. Wool was no longer king, but, as the population of England continued to increase rapidly, sheep were raised for meat rather than fleece. Gloucestershire's Cotswold rams and ewes were once again in demand.

The sun plays fanciful tricks as it lingers on the mellow stones of this unique landscape. From town to village, it sparkles on the winding roadways and rambling streams. It warms the woolly backs of the grazing sheep that nibble the grass, keeping it low and even across the horizon. And when it breaks through the clouds to smile on the stones and sheep that embody the gentleness of this rural realm, there is no lovelier sight.

Stanton Today

One of the most colorful Cotswold villages is Stanton. The stone here is of an intense hue that glows like burnished copper. The best of the centuries resides in the dwellings that line the steep main road. Standing side by side, framed in dazzling flower gardens, they ascend the hill to the top of the village. Most date from the early 1600s, an era when the local farmers and wool merchants thrived.

In the eighteenth century, the once-vibrant village went into a serious decline. Maintaining the beauty and vitality of these small, out-of-the-way villages takes the energy and imagination of new generations. Stanton was revived and renewed by Philip Stott when he became lord of the manor in 1906, and the beauty of the present-day village stems from his dedication to preservation and careful rebuilding.

Stott, an architect, purchased 882 acres which encompassed most of the village. He immediately set about restoring the buildings, completing a reservoir, and installing lights along the main road that were powered by a generator from his own home, Stanton Court. Through his efforts, the village school was enlarged and a swimming pool and cricket field were built.

The village church of St. Michael and All Angels stands in a serene churchyard just steps north of the quiet main road. It dates from 1100 and is built in the Norman style, though there most likely was a church on the site prior to this time as indicated by King Kenulf of Mercia granting tithes, the Manor and patronage of Stanton to the monks of Winchcombe Abbey in 811. Through the generosity of Sir Philip, the noted church architect Ninian Comper designed the rood screen, the reredos with alabaster figures of the Virgin Mary, St. Peter, St. Michael and St. Barnabas in back of the altar, and the two windows in the east wall of the transepts. The windows are marked with his distinctive strawberry plant symbol. Comper signed his work with a beautiful vine, flower and berry device in memory of his father, the Reverend John Comper, who died in an Aberdeen, Scotland, park while sharing strawberries with a group of poor children.

John Wesley, the founder of Methodism, was a frequent visitor to St. Michael's and preached from its seventeenth-century pulpit. Vestiges of old stone benches used by elderly and ailing parishioners line the south wall near the doorway. And since sheepdogs always accompanied their masters everywhere, the wooden sides of the medieval pews at the nave's northwest end are deeply scarred by the chains that restrained the dogs during church services. In 1939, following the deaths of Sir Philip and Lady Stott, the Lady Chapel was restored and dedicated in their memory.

Stanton Court sits at the lower, northwest end of the village. It is a splendid example of Jacobean architecture surrounded by extensive grounds and stunning gardens. The Mount Inn, by contrast, occupies a spot to the northeast near the top of the main road. It offers glorious views of the surrounding fields where sheep still graze as they have for centuries.

Finding Your Way

Stanton is about eleven miles northeast of Cheltenham on the B4632. Turn south at the sign for Stanton and drive about three-quarters of a mile to the village.

Nearby Places of Interest

Stanway House, about a mile south of Stanton, has an elaborate seventeenth-century gatehouse which displays the arms of the Tracy family over its magnificent entrance. It is Jacobean in style and filled with ancestral portraits and fine antique furniture. Ancient oaks shade the grounds and meadows near the house. A recently restored water garden features a canal and fountain. The fourteenth-century tithe barn is an excellent example of medieval structural design. Its impressive stone roof sits on cruck timbers. There is also a cricket pavilion. The church of St. Peter, with its Victorian refurbishments, can be found near the gatehouse.

Snowshill, directly east of Stanton, can be reached by heading north in the direction of Broadway and driving south on the road signposted for Snowshill. It is a Cotswold treasure. The manor house is a National Trust property and contains unique objects collected by Charles Wade because of their finely crafted construction. Toys, clocks, and superbly-woven tapestries are displayed next to body armor and intricate marine instruments. There is even a room devoted entirely to wheels of various sizes. Terraced gardens shimmer with flowering trees near rock-walled beds overflowing with bright blossoms. A Norman church occupies the small green across from the pub and lovely stone cottages angle into the hillside. Steep roads twist and turn down into the lush valley or up onto the windswept wolds.

Chipping Campden, about eight miles northeast of Stanton, was one of the richest of the medieval wool towns. Today, it is a bustling place with a broad High Street edged with perfectly proportioned, golden buildings. The Market Hall in the town's center was built in 1627. The splendid perpendicular church of St. James with its beautifully crafted tower and Sir Baptist Hicks' 1613 gatehouse, all that is left of his mansion which was destroyed in the English Civil War, reflect the wealth and glory of the town. There is a variety of craft workshops, as well as a collection of photos and drawings relating the history of the village and the local arts and crafts movement at the Silk Mill in Sheep Street. A mile to the northwest, the natural amphitheater on Dover's Hill looks out over the idyllic Vale of Evesham.

Hidcote Manor Gardens, about four miles northeast of Chipping Campden, is a classic collection of magnificent formal gardens, borders, impeccably trimmed hedges and woodlands that features plants from around the world. Created by an American, Major Lawrence Johnstone, the garden gracefully unfolds with individual displays separated by unique hedge plantings. Exotic varieties of roses, shrubs and trees provide a horticultural extravaganza in one of England's most visited gardens. The nearby hamlets of Hidcote Bartrim and Hidcote Boyce offer wonderful walks near the duck pond and along lanes bordered by attractive thatched cottages.

Winchcombe *(See Chapter 4)*

Chapter Two

The Eastleachs

The

Country Pub

To find an out-of-the-way village, walk its leafy lanes and flower-embroidered footpaths, and come across a comfortable pub along the way is like discovering a little piece of traveler's paradise.

The communal sharing of food and drink for a price is an ancient custom. When the Romans came to Britain, they built their roads and established "tabernae" along the way so travelers could restore themselves with wine. The ale-drinking Saxons, who followed, lived in small groups and rarely traveled great distances. The Roman roads—and taverns—fell into disuse. Eventually, as the Saxon kingdoms grew, alehouses sprang up along the rivers and roads that crossed each domain.

Early monasteries often included inns that offered food and lodging to weary wayfarers. When the Normans arrived in 1066, monastic expansion flourished, and they built magnificent shrines to honor the saints. Establishments between these pilgrimage sites did brisk business.

Post houses kept horses for royal messengers to use when they traveled on official business. These designated inns also attracted other travelers and became strategic points to pick up and drop off mail. By the time carriages regularly transported travelers cross-country, many inns along the growing network of highways had expanded in grand style. Even though these public houses and inns catered to the transient trade, villages and towns off the main roadways maintained their own pubs for the local population.

In the early days, straightforward, easy-to-understand signs attracted customers. Across the empire, Romans traditionally hung a cluster of vine leaves over a door as an indication that wine was available for sale. These leaves were uncommon in Britain, so a small, green bush became the mark of this early hospitality.

Alehouses displayed poles or alestakes. These were simple places, often the extension of a dwelling, where the goodwife brewed enough drink for her family and some to sell on the side. Most people drank ale. Wine was rare and expensive, and sanitation was so poor that water sources couldn't always be trusted.

The first signboards used symbols with religious significance such as a star or cross. As time passed, they incorporated the coat of arms of the landlord whose land they occupied or an emblem relating to royalty: Three Crowns, Rose and Crown, Red Lion, The Castle. Rough images like a shepherd or ferryboat depicted local occupations. Animals were, and still are, popular names for pubs: Black Bull, The Swan, Goat's Head or King Richard II's symbol White Hart, portraying a stag often with golden antlers.

During the decades when stagecoaches careened across the country, another practice entered the culture. Passengers paid more for seats inside the coach. Upon reaching an inn, these travelers were invited into the proprietor's salon. Those that rode on the top of the coach went to the public bar to drink while the horses were changed and the driver prepared to continue the journey. In the years that followed, the private area came to be called the lounge bar and the public bar offered drinks and entertainment to a very different clientele. Remnants of this distinction are still seen today in the physical layout of many pubs with lounges on one side and the public bar on the other.

The rich heritage of the public house is celebrated in the congeniality of a sociable drink with friends new and old. Polished wood hand pumps mounted on the bar bringing beer up from the barrels in the cellar, and the smooth tables and comfortable chairs are a long way from the rough, unrefined ancient alehouse atmosphere, but refreshment remains the primary objective.

Topping the traditional pub menu are Steak and Kidney Pie, Fish and Chips, or Bangers and Mash, a sausage that bursts—bang!—if the cook neglects to pierce it, served with a generous dollop of potatoes. Vegetarian dishes and more elaborate offerings have been popularized in recent years. Pub food generally delivers large portions and good value for money spent. A full complement of drinks is now served, though most regulars agree nothing beats a perfectly-pulled pint.

The surroundings are pleasant and inviting. Colorful hanging plants often decorate the entrance, soaking up the last rays of sunshine on a long summer's evening. Logs blaze and crackle on the hearth, taking the chill out of a damp winter's night. A dart board generally takes pride of place at the end of the barroom. The origins of this traditional pub game go back hundreds of years when it was played as a form of archery. It is said that passengers on the Mayflower brought the game with them to the New World, and after World War II, its popularity spread across the globe. Though tournament play follows set rules, there are many variations on the way the game—some say sport—is played. Dominoes are another favorite pub pastime, as well as Skittles, a ninepins bowling game played with a ball or wooden disk.

Through the centuries taverns, alehouses, inns and pubs have offered food, drink and accommodation in various combinations. They have always been a central place for meeting, greeting, exchanging news and expounding on personal views. From the top to the bottom of the country, east to west, the institution of the public house remains happily and historically entrenched in British custom and society.

Eastleach Turville and
Eastleach Martin Today

Thickly-plaited hedgerows keep travelers in suspense until they crest a hill and descend toward the Eastleachs. Special, tucked-away places, Eastleach Turville and Eastleach Martin offer natural splendor to those lucky enough to uncover their simple beauty. They are separated by the River Leach but connected by Keble's Bridge, a rare clapper bridge made from several broad, flat stone slabs resting on rough pillars that form a walk across the water. The mossy banks of the river are dressed in willow finery and reeds bend down to touch their reflections as the cool water swirls past.

As the scene unfolds, a picturesque stone house with a stately tower displaying a gold, Roman-numeraled clock face comes into view. There is an old pub on the hill, a lovely manor in the distance, and since each area came under the auspices of different landowners, two churches. The narrow road passes by these lovely landmarks and loops back across the river, sidestepping cheerful gardens and a stout, stone and wood corral where a shaggy miniature pony thrusts his head through the rails to say hello. Or maybe he's suggesting a stop at the pub followed by a relaxing stroll along the river.

A sign proclaiming the name of the pub and a profile of the queen is mounted over the entrance to the Victoria. Creeper vines scale the honey-colored stone exterior reaching for the baskets of flowers that light up either side of the front door. When the weather turns cool, the attractive interior is warmed by a welcoming fire. Its dancing light reflects in the brass and burnished wood. Behind the bar, red-coated horsemen chase the hounds on the beautifully painted hand pulls that dispense beer into tall glasses. Daily specials are chalked on a board for diners to consider. The Victoria is not the oldest pub in the district, but its mellow, understated charm is well-suited to its tranquil surroundings.

The Keble family came into possession of the manor of Eastleach Turville in the sixteenth century. John Keble, the noted poet who had considerable influence on the Church of England in the nineteenth century, was a founding member of the Oxford Movement. Keble College at Oxford University is named for him. He served as non-resident curate of St. Andrew's at Turville and St. Michael and St. Martin church at Eastleach Martin in 1815. Both churches are constructed in the Norman style with simple, architecturally beautiful interiors and peaceful, country churchyards.

Cotswold stone predominates here. There are several cottages surrounded by stands of trees and glimpses of bordering farmland through the greenery. One lovely home near St. Andrew's gazes out over a delicately carved topiary hedge. This enthralling landscape is best explored on foot. The river doesn't really separate these two captivating areas; it unites them in an undeniably idyllic scene to be admired from both sides.

Finding Your Way

Eastleach Turville and neighboring Eastleach Martin are about thirteen miles northeast of Cirencester. Follow the A417 east from Cirencester. At Fairford, take the signposted road northeast to Southrop. Continue north to the Eastleachs.

Nearby Places of Interest

St. Mary's Church, Fairford, approximately ten miles east of Cirencester, is one of the great wool churches of the region. A prosperous wool merchant, John Tame, rebuilt St. Mary's Church in the perpendicular style. It is notable for its complete set of twenty-eight medieval windows that depict the basis of the Christian faith in glorious stained glass dating from 1500-1517. These incredible glass panels were used like a book to teach the largely illiterate population about the Bible and the life of Christ. The windows were removed and stored during the Civil War and World War II to safeguard the glass. John Tame's tomb, with its brass top, is located between the chancel and the Lady Chapel. There are intricately carved misericords in the chancel. Monks had to stand while singing the prayers and hymns of the daily services. The misericords, "tip-up seats," provided support and allowed them to lean back while still remaining on their feet. The St. Mary's misericords are thought to have come from Cirencester Abbey following Henry VIII's Dissolution of the Monasteries. They are heavily carved with scenes from the Old Testament and folktales. Delicately sculpted statues adorn the outside of the building, and the figure of a mischievous boy scaling the wall looks down on the churchyard from his spot above the third window to the right of the church porch. Tiddles, a favorite church cat, has a small stone monument in the churchyard.

అ అ అ

Lechlade, about four miles south of Eastleach Turville and Eastleach Martin, is named for the River Leach. It is here that the Leach and Coln rivers come together and flow with the Thames. Stone for the rebuilding of St. Paul's Cathedral was quarried at nearby Taynton and shipped by river from Lechlade to London. Today, pleasure boats are the primary traffic on the river. St. Lawrence Church stands proudly near the market square. It is this churchyard, near the Thames, that Shelley immortalized in his poem *Summer Evening Meditation.* The church is built in the perpendicular style and dates from the late fifteenth century. Brasses in the floor of the north aisle memorialize the wool merchant John Townsend and his wife Ellen. There is another brass dedicated to Robert Hichman. Some of the pillars in the nave are etched with mason's marks. The chancel features fifteenth-century roof bosses, with a photograph on the north wall of the sanctuary explaining their meaning. The exterior of the tower is adorned with curious carved heads located under the battlements. St. John's Bridge was constructed in 1229 and next to it stands an old stone pub, The Trout. In the garden, there are remnants of a priory that once stood on the site. The town offers a variety of attractive walks in and around the bustling market square, across the bridges and along the banks and tranquil water meadows.

ю   ю   ю

Southrop, a little over a mile to the south of the Eastleachs, has a small green, a charming collection of cottages and the village church where John Keble once served as curate. He lived at the Old Vicarage and Oxford students would attend reading parties there. To gain entrance to the local pub, The Swan, visitors must duck under heavy vines that completely cover the outside. In autumn, the vine leaves turn a brilliant, blazing red adding even more character to the building which dates from 1645.

ю   ю   ю

Little Barrington, about four miles north of the Eastleachs, is a small cluster of golden stone buildings bordering a broad village green. The cottages are softened by stands of trees and bright, open fields. The Strongs, a local family of master stone masons, supplied the stone for many beautiful houses throughout the Cotswolds. Quarried stone traveled on barges down the nearby Windrush River on its way to London for the rebuilding of the city after the Great Fire of 1666. The village Church of St. Peter stands in a peaceful churchyard at the end of a small lane. Scenic spots along the glistening river look across to neighboring Great Barrington.

జి   జి   జి

Northleach *(See Chapter 3)*
Chedworth *(See Chapter 6)*

Chapter Three

Northleach

Memorialized in Brass

The peaceful precincts of a church, whether a magnificent cathedral or simple country place of prayer, relate the stories of the centuries through its silent memorials. There is no need for spoken words. Written inscriptions confirm the living and passing of individuals and families in names, dates and so much more. Some are elaborate with long, rhyming epitaphs and artistic workmanship. Lustrous marble reflects the jewel tones of towering stained glass windows. Many more are modestly embossed like the plainly engraved floor stones that absorb the footsteps of worshippers and sightseers alike.

In the twelfth century, memorials began to take on increased importance. Loved ones were commemorated, the nobility and clergy glorified. Though most people encountering monuments couldn't read the dedications on the graves, it was hoped they would be inclined to say a brief prayer for the deceased in whose memory the tomb had been erected.

Memorial brasses added an interesting facet to these final resting places. They were less vulnerable to age-related deterioration than stone and, therefore, provided a more resilient, longer lasting monument. Made from an alloy of copper and zinc with minute amounts of lead and tin, the material called latten was brought to England from the Continent. It was generally imported from Cologne, Germany, and shipped to Britain in large sheets which made the brasses very costly.

When a memorial brass was commissioned, the sheets were pounded into a plate. Commemoratives often featured life-size figures requiring more than one sheet of brass. A mason, employing procedures used by stone carvers, made the engraving. The metal pieces were then fitted onto a stone slab. Set into small recesses chiseled in the stone, borders, text, ornamentation and figure(s) were held in place with pitch and brass nails. Some brasses were accented with colors and adorned with colored enamels.

The Northleach brasses are considered to be among the best examples of commemorative brasses in all of Europe. They serve as memorials to the wool merchants of the parish of St. Peter and St. Paul, often referred to as "The Cathedral of the Cotswolds."

These impressive memorials, while not exact likenesses, reveal the physical characteristics of people who lived in the fifteenth and sixteenth centuries. They chronicle their occupations, social status and provide insight into family life and religious convictions as expressed in the tombs' inscriptions. The collective brasses form a series of creative commentary on people in one specific area of England whose professional interests expanded far beyond the locale in which they lived. These artistically detailed memorials are linked by common elements, but each contributes a unique chapter to the story that has had a lasting impact on the town of Northleach.

The oldest of the brasses bears the date 1400. It honors a woolman and his wife, though their names are not known. The male figure is dressed in a long garment cinched by a highly carved belt from which hangs a dagger. A woolpack beneath his feet indicates his profession. Though the top of his head is bald, the hair around the ears is clipped close. His chin is covered with a forked beard. Her floor-length dress, with small buttons at the wrist and neck, is partially covered by a long cape. A veil hides the hair and drapes gracefully on her shoulders. Companionably, a little dog sits amid the folds at the hem of her dress.

Another brass depicts Agnes and her husbands, William Scors and Thomas Fortey. William Scors was a tailor, and scissors rest between his feet. The intricately worked border contains an inscription referring to Thomas Fortey as well as illustrations of roses, lilies, geese, dogs and other animals similar to those that appear in manuscripts from the era. The two men are dressed in robes that reach to just above their ankles. Agnes is slightly shorter than her husbands. The folds of her gown reach the floor. The dates are worthy of special attention. William's death date is 1420 and appears entirely in Roman Numerals. The year of Thomas' death, 1447, is written in a combination of Roman and Arabic numerals. The 47 is slanted differently than the number appears in modern writing, but it is thought to be one of the earliest incorporations of Arabic numerals on a memorial brass. Agnes' name is followed by a 14. Memorials were often made within a person's lifetime, the year engraved later as dictated by a surviving relative or friend. On this marker, Agnes' death date is left incomplete.

John Fortey is credited with much of the fifteenth-century rebuilding of St. Peter and St. Paul Church and left a large sum of money in his will to ensure the work could be completed. His tribute is engraved with the date 1458 and resides in the north arcade close to the pulpit. Hands steepled in prayer, he has a sheep under his right foot and a woolpack under the left. His hair is worn short, and there is no mustache or beard. Each of the six medallions bordering the brass shows his woolmark. This mark would have been stamped on all the goods he sent to market. He is the only figure depicted on the monument. By contrast, John Taylour is surrounded by his wife Joan and their fifteen children. Also a woolman, Taylour wears his hair long and his shoes are wide rather than pointed, indicating a significant change in style during the thirty-two years between Fortey's death and Taylour's demise in 1490.

A brass attributed to William Midwinter indicates he died in 1500 followed by his wife a year later. Their feet rest on sheep and woolpacks signifying they were both wool merchants. The figures of Robert and Anne Serche look toward each other on their brass. Three sons are dressed just like their father, and the daughter wears the same style gown and headdress as her mother. The date, 1501, is expressed in a unique combination of stylized Roman Numerals and the word "one."

The engraved canopies over the heads of Thomas and Joan Bushe bear renderings of shields and different breeds of sheep. This couple also died one year apart—Thomas in 1525 and Joan in 1526. The symbolic sheep and woolpack are pictured beneath both his feet and hers. The elaborate decoration attests to their earthly success while the inscription humbly requests prayers for their eternal souls.

Among the remaining brasses are those of a former vicar William Lawnder who died in 1530, and a medallion and children's figures which are all that survive of William and Margaret Bicknell's memorial. Maud Parker Thomas, whose acrostic poem combines the letters of her name with her husband's on a brass in the Lady Chapel, tells of her devotion to God, family and community.

Monumental brasses were systematically defaced and stripped from their original placements during the Reformation. The valuable materials were reworked by engravers who used the plain sides to fashion new memorials. The Civil War also had a devastating impact on the brasses. The austere Puritans removed many of the commemoratives. In addition, items made of metal were confiscated and used for different purposes to further the cause of each side in the conflict.

The remarkable brass memorials of St. Peter and St. Paul Church have remained relatively untouched. They are an important element of the country's heritage and an extraordinary historical record for future generations.

Northleach Today

A wrought iron sign, artistically emblazoned with a sheep standing on a woolpack, welcomes visitors to the Cotswold town of Northleach. The signpost proudly calls attention to the town's long trading tradition by announcing it was granted an annual market charter in 1227.

Trade routes and major roadways have always crisscrossed the area around Northleach. About 300 B.C., an Iron Age track wound its way through the Leach River valley. The great Fosse Way, of Roman origin, passes along the west end of town. And just south of town, packhorses carried precious cargo from the Droitwich salt mines along the Salt Way. When the Abbey of Gloucester established the market town of Northleach, eighty parcels of land were marked off to the north and south of the marketplace. These burgage plots, though some have been combined to form larger holdings, and the triangular marketplace are the essence of the modern-day town.

Small shops, the post office and old lockup curve around the marketplace toward the Sherbourne Arms pub. Behind the pub lies the village green, bordered by two half-timbered houses. Tudor House, now an art gallery, is traditionally referred to as the house where the wool merchant John Fortey lived. Close by is Mill End where the River Leach spills into the mill pond near the church.

St. Peter and St. Paul is one of the Cotswold's most prominent wool churches. Though the tower dates from before the fourteenth century, many of the present features date from the fifteenth century when the town's wool merchants contributed generously to the expansion and beautification of the sacred structure.

The burnished wood and pale stone interior is illuminated by natural light from its grand clerestory windows. The fifteenth-century pulpit and the font from the previous century are richly carved. Impressive brass monuments dedicated to the woolmen and their families are positioned throughout the church. Contrasting with the fine brasses is a contemporary wall hanging displayed near the children's area. It is made of fine Cotswold wool, hand-dyed with natural materials: parsley, nettles, onion skins, buckthorn, twigs and berries. It is duly noted that the sheep who provided the fleece for this decorative addition to the old church are Sam, Charley, Jacob, Jonah and Jesse.

Along the town's main thoroughfare are buildings bearing charmingly old-fashioned names: Malthouse, Wheatsheaf, King's Head House. Another black and white half-timbered building, a pub called the Red Lion Inn, dates from the sixteenth century. Keith Harding's World of Mechanical Music is a few doors away. It houses an incredible array of self-playing instruments and an impressive collection of music boxes. The Victorian Music Room offers classical music, and a piano from a Berlin café calls to mind the cabaret performances of the 1920s. A world-renowned team of craftsmen are involved in restoration in the workshop.

The impressive stone buildings of Northleach bear witness to the golden days of England's medieval wool trade. The past lives harmoniously with the present in solid, rural beauty.

Finding Your Way

Northleach is located about twelve miles southeast of Cheltenham, just off the A40.

Nearby Places of Interest

Cotswold Heritage Center, less than a mile west of Northleach, is an indoor/outdoor museum of rural life and area history. Displays feature wagons, farm implements, information about rural occupations, and rooms with typical country furnishings. Craftsmen demonstrate age-old skills. Once the site of the House of Correction, visitors can also see a restored cell block and courtroom.

❧   ❧   ❧

Upper and Lower Slaughter, about six miles northeast of Northleach, are two of the most picturesque villages in the Cotswolds. They decorate the banks of the River Eye with their memorable golden buildings of Cotswold stone. A few cottages and farmhouses border the sedate, tree-lined lanes of Upper Slaughter, along with a lovely Elizabethan manor house and the Church of St. Peter, built in the Norman style. The church was severely damaged during the Civil War, but survived through the years and saw extensive restoration work in the late nineteenth century. The road from the church winds steeply down to a stone bridge where the signposted Warden's Way leads visitors through restful open fields of grazing sheep to the village of Lower Slaughter, barely a mile away. Lower Slaughter's 1880 water mill, once a corn mill, is now a museum with ice cream parlor, tea room, gift and craft shops. Its wheel churns steadily as ducks skitter along the water and pad noisily across the stone bridges of the village. St. Mary's Church dates from medieval times, but was rebuilt in 1866. Passing by a manor house with a lovely sixteenth-century dovecote and garden, flower-filled lanes ramble through the village and bend along the edges of the river.

❧   ❧   ❧

The Eastleachs *(See Chapter 2)*
Chedworth *(See Chapter 6)*

Chapter Four

Winchcombe

Queen

Katherine Parr

Anne lifted the skirt of her black dress as she stepped quietly over the threshold and into the room. She reached down into the cradle and patted the small pillow where the subtle imprint of the infant Mary's head had left a shallow indentation. Smoothing the rich fabric of the quilt, she slowly glanced around the nursery. The baby's mother had chosen well. Everything in the magnificent room spoke of elegance and beauty.

Moving to the window, her eyes scanned the garden below. The feathery edges of the herbs seemed to droop slightly in the warmth of the midday sun. The vistas beyond the nursery glass appeared lifeless, without color or vitality.

There was such gaiety here just a few short months ago when she arrived with the other ladies-in-waiting who were part of the dowager queen Katherine Parr's huge entourage. Thomas Seymour, Lord of Sudeley, proudly escorted his new bride to the exquisite private apartments his carpenters and stonemasons had built for her. Maids of honor and serving women hurried through the castle corridors, preparing the sun-filled rooms. Sir Thomas, recently appointed Lord High Admiral of England, dealt with streams of horsemen who rode in and out of the courtyard carrying messages from all corners of the realm. The old castle came to life again with the arrival of the Seymours.

Sudeley Castle had almost fallen into ruin in recent years, but when Henry VIII died, his son, Edward VI, granted the estates to Seymour. Sir Thomas, the new king's uncle, was the brother of Jane Seymour, Henry's third wife and the young King Edward's mother.

Katherine and Thomas first met at the court of Henry VIII. She had married at seventeen and was widowed twice by the time she was thirty. Upon her second husband's death, she became deeply involved with Seymour. But the king also sought her company. She turned away from Seymour, and Henry, anxious to marry again, made Katherine his sixth wife. During the three-and-a-half years they spent as husband and wife, she nursed the aging king, entertained him—sharing his passionate interest in music—and acted as stepmother to his three children.

While Katherine was consort to Henry, Seymour continued to involve himself in the dangerous intrigues of the day. He had powerful connections and ambitiously sought influence and wealth for himself, even to the point of paying court to Henry's daughters, the princesses Mary and Elizabeth, each destined one day to be queen in her own right. Within a few short weeks of Henry's death, he renewed his relationship with Katherine, proposed to her and was accepted.

In the days that followed her arrival at Sudeley, Katherine began to make the castle her home. She prepared, with great anticipation, for the birth of her first child. The nursery chambers were decorated with elegant fabrics, finely woven tapestries, and splendid, gilded furnishings. She prayed daily in St. Mary's Chapel and walked in the grounds, often conferring with her young companion, Lady Jane Grey. Jane had come to court at the age of nine and remained under the guardianship of Katherine who brought her to Sudeley. Their relationship was one of great affection, and the intellectually precocious Jane learned a great deal from the accomplished Katherine.

On August 30, 1548, Katherine's daughter Mary was born and welcomed with great joy and happiness. The nursemaids cared for her every need, and Katherine was left to rest and recover. But on the third day, the thirty-six-year-old mother contracted puerperal—childbed—fever. Within a few days, the infection took her life.

Anne turned from the beautiful bower window. Pressing her hands to the sides of her face, she experienced again the profound loss of her vivacious mistress. It was hard to accept that she was gone. Closing her eyes, she struggled to banish images of the solemn funeral procession: masses of black cloth draped throughout the chapel; the slow steps of the chief mourner, Lady Jane Grey, so young to bear the loss of her dear friend and guardian; the voice of Miles Coverdale, the great cleric of the Reformation, translator of the Bible, as he sorrowfully spoke the words of the funeral sermon. She felt renewed shock at the memory of Thomas Seymour, eager to return to London, departing Sudeley before his wife's funeral.

The door opened and the rustle of the nursemaid's skirts, coupled with little Mary's soft whimpers, brought Anne from her reverie. She reached out and stroked the child's soft, round cheek, a simple gesture of comfort her own mother could not provide.

Returning to London, Anne heard that Seymour had been charged with treason and condemned to die by beheading. The outcome of Thomas Seymour's trial did not surprise her. Even she was aware of his callous plots to discredit the king's protector and gain more control over the young Edward. His scheme to marry Lady Jane Grey to Edward, among other intrigues and maneuverings, proved to be his undoing. The death sentence was duly carried out on Tower Hill on March 20, 1549.

Anne often thought of the child Mary, now without a mother or father. Katherine Parr's daughter was living with Katherine, Duchess of Suffolk. At least her father had spared a thought for her well-being before his death and made arrangements for her care.

Sudeley Castle, where the infant spent her first days, passed to other owners in rapid succession. These were capricious times. The country was in turmoil, and nobles were quickly in and out of favor. Anne never visited the golden stone castle again, but she was forever haunted by tragic recollections of Mary Seymour's birth, Katherine Parr's untimely death, and the child's unknown destiny.

Winchcombe Today

The narrow streets of modern-day Winchcombe stretch in every direction. Their names reflect the ancient Saxon capital of Mercia's long history. When the great Benedictine Abbey was completely destroyed at the time of Henry VIII's Dissolution of the Monasteries, the stones were used to construct many of the buildings in the town.

Outside the town hall, the current visitor's center and Folk and Police Museum, stand the old seven-hole stocks. Local lore claims the odd hole was used for the town's one-legged lawbreaker. Across the street is the George Inn, now called the George Mews, which sheltered pilgrims visiting Hailes and Winchcombe Abbeys. The pilgrims' gallery can be seen through the doorway arch.

Winchcombe was the site of great horse fairs held each year in March and July. Iron rings, still in evidence along North Street, were used to tether horses during these events. Treacle Mary is named for Mary Yiend. She once sold sweets and cakes in her quaint North Street shop. Continuing down Gloucester Street, Cowl Lane is lined with private residences that were once domestic buildings attached to Winchcombe Abbey. Where small gardens cheerfully bloom and trees present seasonal flowers, abbey monks walked in the shadows of the lane with their cowls pulled up over their heads.

The parish Church of St. Peter dates from 1468, and its tower stands ninety feet high, topped by a gilded weathercock. The exterior walls of the church display forty "grotesques." These stone carvings represent demons and what might be the faces of important people associated with the fifteenth-century town and abbey. Standing in the corner of the churchyard is a preacher's cross which commemorates the diamond jubilee of Queen Victoria. Fittingly, a statue of St. Peter guards the entrance to the church. During nineteenth-century excavations on the site of Winchcombe Abbey, a pair of stone coffins was uncovered. They now rest at the west end of the nave and are thought to contain the remains of King Kenulf of Mercia who died in 821, and his son, St. Kenelm. There is a long legend attached to the murder of the boy Kenelm whose memory brought many pilgrims to the abbey. A medieval oak screen conceals the choir vestry. Among its fine decorations is the Winchcombe Imp who stares out from the third opening on the left. The magnificent altar cloth attributed to Catherine of Aragon while she stayed at Sudeley Castle is displayed near the north door. It features her distinctive pomegranate symbol.

Down a narrow passageway at Number 23 Gloucester Street is the Winchcombe Railway Museum. It houses one of England's most complete collections of rail equipment with many interactive exhibits. A garden filled with rare plants adjoins the museum. Further down the street, on the corner of Malthouse Lane, is the Corner Cupboard Inn, once a farmhouse, said to be haunted by the ghost of a young girl.

Turning into Vineyard Street, fine stone cottages stand side by side. The steep incline, once known as Duck Street, leads to the River Isbourne where the ducking stool was employed to silence town gossips. This is the way to Sudeley Castle.

The peaceful valley in which the castle stands is splashed with the vivid textures of wandering wildflowers and mighty oaks. The original manor was a tenth-century wedding gift, but Ralph Boteler embarked on a massive building project in the mid-fifteenth century to transform Sudeley into a castle befitting his high rank. It has survived many tragedies and the ravages of political conflict. Sudeley has been restored with great dedication and imagination, and its colorful history can be revisited in the beautiful rooms and splendid gardens.

The rooms of the castle exude great warmth. Personal portraits and rich paneling provide a quiet, understated elegance rather than making a grand statement. Stunning works of art by Van Dyck, Rubens and Turner are displayed with cherished treasures such as Katherine Parr's prayer book, a lock of her hair and painted miniatures of the queen. The nursery she prepared for her daughter survives.

The tithe barn and walls of the banqueting hall remain as ruins glorified by a pond, exquisite flower borders and masses of shrubbery. They are the focal point of the view from the castle windows along with the extensive gardens. Roses have a special place at Sudeley. There are multiple varieties, some of which fill the formal parterres in the Queen's Garden enclosed by innovative double yew hedges planted under the supervision of Emma Dent, a nineteenth-century lady of the castle responsible for much of the extensive rebuilding and restoration seen at Sudeley today.

Daisies mark the path that Katherine Parr took to St. Mary's Chapel for her daily devotions. Life-size topiaries of the queen and Lady Jane Grey stand in the White Garden. The queen holds a prayer book copied from the one on display in the castle. There are several memorials within the chapel. It is here, to the left of the altar, that Katherine Parr is buried. She lies beneath an intricately carved canopy with angels watching over her. At the end of the day, when all the visitors to the castle depart, a staff member turns out the lights with a simple, "Good night, Kate."

Finding Your Way

Winchcombe is approximately eight miles northeast of Cheltenham, just off the B4632.

<u>Nearby Places of Interest</u>

Hailes Abbey, about two miles northeast of Winchcombe, was an important pilgrimage site. The Cistercian Abbey, founded by monks brought from Beaulieu Abbey, displayed a small phial they claimed contained the blood of Christ, and pilgrims from across Britain traveled to Hailes to offer their prayers. Though now a ruin, the foundation plan of the church can be clearly seen, and sections of the cloister arches remain standing. Relics from the site, including tiles, stone and pieces from a thirteenth-century effigy, are displayed in the museum.

Belas Knap, approximately two miles southwest of Winchcombe, is an elaborate burial mound with four chambers. This Neolithic long barrow, considered one of Gloucestershire's finest examples of an ancient burial site, has a large forecourt, a false entrance—the actual entries are on the sides of the mound—and extensive drystack walls. Long barrows typically extend in a narrow mound-like fashion. Belas Knap stands more than 13 feet high, 178 feet long, and about 60 feet wide.

Cotswold Farm Park, located about seven miles west of Winchcombe, is home to an amazing variety of animals: Gloucester cattle, Cotswold sheep and rare British breeds.

Visitors can enjoy woodland walks, tractor safaris and daily seasonal demonstrations such as lambing, bottle feeding the youngsters, and sheep shearing. Working animals like oxen and sheepdogs exhibit the talents that make them valuable members of the farm family.

Stanton *(See Chapter 1)*

Chapter Five

Painswick

A Country Churchyard

Lofty silhouettes of yew trees frame entry doors to the church and cast curious shadows across the grass and narrow pathways. The last visitor carefully closes the lych-gate as birds settle into their bell tower nests high above the ground. When evening descends on a country churchyard, a sense of time and modern life fade with the light of day.

History and legend, custom and tradition come together inside the walls of these sacred places. On sites where ancient people once gathered, Christians built their churches and often enclosed the land around them. Stones remaining from the construction of the church proper were sometimes used to shape the boundary walls. In medieval times, these hallowed grounds served as gathering places for the villagers. Church ales—celebrations with dancing, sporting activities and plenty of ale—were held. Miracle plays and dramatizations of biblical stories and episodes from the lives of saints took center stage. Now the churchyards stand in near silence, cloaking the country church in soft tufts of long grass, curling tendrils of ivy and seasonal visitations of wildflowers.

Many English churchyards are entered by way of the lych-gate. The gate hinges on the front posts of a rectangular structure that supports a shallow, protective roof. Benches or slabs are built into the sides of the covered area inside the gate. The name comes from the Anglo-Saxon word "lych" for body or corpse. It was the practice for mourners to carry the body of the deceased to the churchyard entrance. They would set the shrouded corpse or coffin down inside the lych-gate until the priest arrived to begin the first part of the burial service.

While generations of ordinary folk were consigned to unmarked graves, people of importance were buried inside the church with stone slabs indicating the locations of their interment. As interior space began to dwindle, burials in the churchyard became more commonplace. It wasn't until the seventeenth century that gravestones and chest tombs—above ground, rectangular, box-like memorials—were commonly erected in memory of the departed. And even then, only the most prosperous families could afford to commission markers.

Typical placement of the oldest exterior monuments is on the south side of the church. When that area was totally occupied, the east and west sides were used. Superstition held that the devil prowled the northern precincts of the churchyard. It was generally the last area to be used for burials.

Masons, who constructed local stone houses and other buildings, usually carved the grave markers. The shapes and sizes of the monuments reflected popular architectural styles of the day. Designs such as the baroque, eighteenth-century chest tombs favored throughout the Cotswolds attested to distinct regional preferences. The work of a particular master mason often appeared repeatedly in specific geographic areas.

Patches of yellow, green and black lichen spread across the old gravestones. Wind and weather have obscured the words on some, but the deeply carved inscriptions of others survive. Messages of mortality were most commonly used early on, accompanied by etchings of skulls or heads with wings characterizing the departing soul. In later centuries, sentiments about salvation and personal accomplishments became part of the commemorative text. Angels benevolently kept their watch, and crosses exemplified eternal faith. The Victorians added iron railings, many of which were removed during World War II to aid the war effort.

Most English country churchyards have at least one pair of yew trees. A yew has the unique ability to stop growing and then regenerate decades later. They often live for hundreds of years and have come, in a spiritual sense, to represent everlasting life. Indigenous to the British Isles, they have long associations with sacred places.

The peaceful atmosphere of a country churchyard attracts creatures great and small. Where neighboring forests have been felled, churchyard trees and shrubbery remain intact, welcoming woodland residents and birds who lend their tuneful songs to the contemplative surroundings. Butterflies sail from flower to flower as the "church" mouse sets up housekeeping in a cranny of the perimeter wall. As the sun sets, all is quiet once again.

Painswick Today

England has had many queens, but only one "Queen of the Cotswolds," as the captivating village of Painswick is called. Her narrow streets and lanes shine with grace and charm as they wind past fourteenth-century buildings, Georgian residences and the churchyard of St. Mary's with its enchanted population of legendary yew trees.

The village is not a sleepy, hidden spot. It retains the town-like feeling of its earlier glory days as a prosperous wool weaving center. Architecturally eye-catching buildings were once homes of affluent clothiers. The weathered, exposed timbers of the old Post Office located on New Street, which was "new" in the 1420s, contrast with the rich Cotswold stone of its neighbors. A Bisley Street house still has its original donkey doors—broad openings to accommodate the animals whose strong backs carried double baskets of wool from the valley mills. Vicarage Street presents views of the surrounding fields dotted with oak, beech trees, and grazing sheep meandering across the meadows at a slow, steady pace.

The lych-gate of St. Mary's Church swings open into a magnificent churchyard filled with impressive rows of towering trees—a spectacular cadre of ninety-nine yews. Legend has it the devil prevents the one-hundredth from taking root. They promenade along pathways around the church and mingle with the myriad of graves and chest tombs that crisscross the churchyard. Most of the trees were planted more than two hundred years ago and are trimmed and skillfully sculpted at the end of every summer, their dense, black-green boughs subdued into shapely ovals and perfect arches.

The tombs, famous for their unique designs and notable masonry, are primarily made of local limestone and date from as early as the seventeenth century. The oldest belongs to William Loveday who died in 1623. Some are ornamented with well preserved copper plates. The striking, hexagonal memorial to Richard Smith has six copper panels engraved with a poetic message. The tombs of William and Christopher Webb indicate they were nurserymen. There is speculation that they may have planted the yew trees. The tombs of the Packer, Palling and Poole families exhibit delicately formed columns, realistic rosettes, highly crafted scrollwork end pieces, and grim, winged skulls. The monument to John Bryan, a carver who died in 1787, stands by itself not far from the lych-gate. He is thought to be the local mason who fashioned many of the surrounding tombs.

The original church was probably built between 1042 and 1066. The structure was expanded during the fourteenth and fifteenth centuries, but the perpendicular spire was not added until 1632. St. Mary's was occupied during the Civil War. Bullet and cannon damage can be seen on the tower walls. An 1883 lightning strike brought a large portion of the tower down into the church building and significant rebuilding was carried out at that time. The south aisle Founder's Window and other windows in the church were designed by Geoffrey Webb and show a spider's web, his signature.

Each year on the Sunday of, or the first Sunday following, September 19, The Clypping Service is held to honor the dedication of the church to the Blessed Virgin Mary. Clypping means enclosing. The ritual observance is carried out by the children of the parish who joyfully join hands and encircle the exterior of the church. They wear flowers and sing celebratory hymns as they move around the building. At the conclusion of the service, each is given a fresh-baked Painswick bun and a silver coin to commemorate the day.

Outside the churchyard are the iron spectacle stocks, resembling a pair of eyeglasses but serving a much more ominous purpose. Criminals were often clapped in stocks positioned near churches in hope that the nearness to consecrated ground would have a positive influence and end the offender's lawbreaking ways.

Visible from a great distance, the spire of St. Mary's church draws attention to Painswick's pleasant position among the steep valleys and dense woodlands of the southern Cotswolds. The Welsh Mountains lie to the west. Visitors who climb to the Iron Age fort at nearby Painswick Beacon are rewarded with a panoramic view of outlying villages and a dazzling visual patchwork of the Severn Valley.

Finding Your Way

Painswick is located about six miles southeast of Gloucester. Follow the B4073 to where it intersects with the A46.

Nearby Places of Interest

Gloucester, approximately six miles northwest of Painswick, is the bustling capital of Gloucestershire. Located on the River Severn, it was known as Glevum in Roman times. Sustaining heavy bomb damage during World War II, Gloucester has many modern districts, but the massive medieval cathedral still dominates the city. The cathedral, originally part of St. Peter's Abbey, dates from 1089. The alabaster effigy of the murdered King Edward II lies atop an elaborate Purbeck marble tomb in the north ambulatory. Following Edward's death at nearby Berkeley Castle in 1327, Gloucester Cathedral became an important pilgrimage site. Its grand east window memorializes the Battle of Crecy. Added in 1349, it is the largest in England. Remarkable fourteenth-century fan vaulting can be seen in the cloisters. Llanthony Warehouse at the historic Gloucester Docks is the site of the National Waterways Museum. The Victorian warehouse features extensive exhibits relating to Britain's canals and waterways. Visitors enter by way of a lock chamber with running water. Narrowboats, barges, and tugboats are displayed. There is a quayside floating exhibit and a machine shop, forge and weighbridge. Decorative objects by canal artists are highlighted in the recently added gallery of Boat Decoration. A diminutive house in College Court is the establishment that inspired Beatrix Potter's sketches for her memorable book *The Tailor of Gloucester*. The house is now a small museum and gift shop.

Painswick Rococo Garden, less than a mile northwest of Painswick, is a splendid restoration of the rococo gardens at Painswick House. Charles Hyett, an asthmatic, built the house because of the good country air and called it Buenos Aires. In the 1740s, his son Benjamin created a magnificent pleasure garden at the back of the house and commissioned Thomas Robins, a local artist, to execute several paintings of the property. By the nineteenth century, the gardens had deteriorated and eventually fell into ruin. The upkeep of the property was enormous, and in 1950 it was converted to woodlands. The rococo period of English gardening spanned a brief forty years from 1720–1760. Dedication to reviving and preserving the historic value of a rare rococo garden led to the intensive Painswick restoration project. Today, the six-acre area features the geometric kitchen garden with its water pool, a plunge pool which is fed by a nearby natural spring, the uniquely designed Red House made of traditional lime plaster washed in an astonishing shade of crimson, and other features detailed in the original Thomas Robins paintings. The garden is brimming with plant varieties that would have been available in the eighteenth century. Spectacular displays of snowdrops show their bright blooms in February and March, and wildlife fills the garden with activity throughout the year.

Owlpen Manor, about ten miles southwest of Painswick, is near the quiet village of Uley. Sheltering under the edge of the steep Cotswold hills, its magnificent collection of manorial buildings is surrounded by lyrically beautiful gardens and tall, protective yew trees. The Church of the Holy Cross stands silently above the manor house which looks out over the tranquil valley and rolling farm fields. In the ninth century, Olla, a Saxon thane, settled the land and from his time more than a thousand years of continuous occupation are documented in the history of the estate. In 1471, prior to her War of the Roses defeat at the Battle of Tewksbury, Queen Margaret of Anjou, wife of Henry VI, stayed at Owlpen. Her ghost is said to return to the manor where she spent her last happy hours before the sad days of her widowhood and exile in France. Owlpen was abandoned for most of the nineteenth century, painstakingly restored in the early twentieth century and is now a family home once again. The church, manor house and gardens are open to view. The old "cyder" house has been transformed into a restaurant, and accommodations are available in the manor house and various cottages on the estate. Lovely walks abound along peaceful country lanes that cross the hills of the almost-hidden hamlet.

తు తు తు

Winchcombe *(See Chapter 4)*
Chedworth *(See Chapter 6)*

Chapter Six

Chedworth

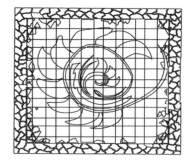

The

Roman Influence

An intricate piece of the British historical tapestry is woven from contributions made by the Romans as early as the first century A.D. The imprint of their advanced engineering knowledge is seen throughout the land: long, straight roads, elaborate baths built near natural springs, organized street plans, bridges and fortified cities.

Society, prior to the arrival of the Romans, existed in small, distinct communities. Celtic clans farmed the land, raised animals, and preserved traditions by passing their oral history from one generation to the next. They kept to themselves when they weren't warring with neighboring tribes. Subdued by the Romans, most Celtic farmers continued to maintain their rural lifestyle after the invasion.

The Roman military enlarged some of these settlements as they advanced across Britannia, creating a vast road system to accommodate troop movements and increased trade. They also established new towns and infused daily life with their ideas and customs.

The population increased. Commerce flourished. Houses and farmsteads were built in the countryside near the towns. The Romans used the word "villa" to describe these houses and their surrounding farm buildings. Residences, constructed in the classic Roman style, featured tiled roofs, decorative mosaics and hypocausts—advanced, sub-floor heating systems. Bathhouses and storehouses occupied land near the main dwelling, and there were usually numerous buildings to accommodate workers involved in the business of the estate. Most domains focused on agriculture. New planting methods and improved tools allowed farmers to increase crop production. Refining skills that existed before the invasion, other villas incorporated Roman techniques and equipment to increase commercial production of pottery and metalwork.

Cirencester, known in Roman times as Corinium, was a frontier outpost that evolved into a thriving Roman town. The town was enclosed by protective walls with good roads leading to and from the market center. It had houses, a forum, shops, and an amphitheater. By the second century, the surrounding land was populated by prosperous, Romanized Britons who had established their households in villas situated on large landholdings. The remains of one of these villas was discovered centuries later at nearby Chedworth.

In 1864, while making his rounds, a gamekeeper came across pieces of strange looking tiles and broken pottery. James Farrer, on behalf of the landowner, the Earl of Eldon, examined the findings and began a two-year excavation, uncovering extensive foundations, walls and building materials. When the initial exploration came to an end, the earl built an on-site museum and had protective roofs placed over the extraordinary archaeological findings.

Digging continued periodically through the following years, unearthing a child's coffin and additional rooms. Painstaking work established that the original living quarters had been enlarged several times over almost three centuries of occupation.

Tucked away on a steep hillside, the earliest villa was a collection of simple buildings overlooking the broad Coln valley. A natural spring on the site probably attracted the first owners to the secluded location. As more rooms were added to the villa, the land was terraced down the slope, and passages with stairs connected the various levels. By the fourth century, the villa residence had reached a size and appearance of uncommon splendor. There were two beautifully ornamented dining rooms, two kitchens, two sophisticated bath suites, a latrine, a garden courtyard and lovely verandas. Vivid mosaics covered the floors. Using local materials, these were generally designed and installed by craftsmen who lived and worked in the area, or by travelers trained in the art of tile-setting based on patterns used throughout the Roman Empire. Near the villa's northwest corner, a columned structure housing the spring's source served as a shrine to the water goddesses.

The Romans were noted for their elaborate bathing rituals, and Romano-British villas incorporated this tradition into suites featuring both damp and dry heat. Baths provided a social setting, not just an opportunity to cleanse and refresh. As they purified their bodies, bathers carried on conversations and even played dice and board games.

Marvels of engineering, the damp and dry suites consisted of rooms arranged at two separate locations within the Chedworth villa complex. Furnaces, stoking chambers, fuel storage areas, flues and extensive piping provided the required heat and water for these multi-room bathing areas.

The Roman military withdrew from Britain at the beginning of the fifth century. In the following decades, trading declined. Marauding invaders and the ravages of plague severely reduced the population. The once-magnificent villas near Corinium fell into disrepair and were abandoned. As the Chedworth villa's walls crumbled, soil from the surrounding hillsides slowly eroded, sliding over the remains. Nature sowed seeds of dense vegetation, patiently reclaiming the site. The villa slept in peace for hundreds of years until further evidence of Rome's impact on Britain's way of life surfaced once again.

Chedworth Today

Narrow country roads wind through sizeable farms, the patterns of their broad fields marked out in perfect, drystack stone walls. Life is peaceful. Sheep graze and the River Coln meanders across the fertile valley floor. Chedworth's mellow stone buildings, most dating from the sixteenth through the eighteenth centuries, decorate the lanes near St. Andrew's Church which has occupied the site since around the twelfth century. Its most striking features are the perpendicular windows that flood the nave with light. The quiet churchyard is adorned with neatly clipped topiary hedges. Chedworth Wood is about a mile from the village. Well-worn walking paths cut through the deep forest to the edge of the villa excavation. The neighboring village of Yanworth offers road access to the villa site.

The real attraction of this pleasing rural landscape is its natural beauty and the recollections of early Roman life as exemplified at the Chedworth Roman Villa. It is one of the finest examples of Romano-British villa reconstruction in all of Great Britain.

The Chedworth Roman Villa is in the care of the National Trust. The visitor's center presents an informative fifteen-minute film about the arrival of the Romans in the area, followed by fascinating facts detailing the archaeological work carried out to-date at the Chedworth site. Entering the excavation, the villa's symmetrical design immediately comes into view. Exposed foundations and walls of various heights give an indication of the villa's size in the fourth century.

The original museum, built in Victorian times when the dig was started, still occupies the center of the excavated area. Changes at the villa are well-documented by aerial photography and comprehensive drawings. Mosaics, local and imported pottery, pieces of painted plaster, coins, iron tools, small altars decorated with images of pagan gods as well as stones bearing a Christian symbol are on display.

The extensive remnants of the baths are particularly impressive. It is easy to imagine bathers passing through the warm, hot and cold rooms, enjoying the ritual damp or dry-heat experience.

More than twenty villas have been discovered within a ten-mile radius of Chedworth Roman Villa. Future archaeological investigations will undoubtedly expand the knowledge of what life was like during this important era of British history.

Finding Your Way

Chedworth is about ten miles northeast of Cirencester. Follow the A429 from Cirencester in the direction of Northleach. Approximately seven miles northeast of Cirencester, at Fossebridge, follow the signs to Yanworth. Chedworth Roman Villa is signposted along the way.

Nearby Places of Interest

Cirencester, approximately ten miles southwest of Chedworth, is the capital of the region and once occupied a place of great significance along the important trade and military routes carved out by the Roman master builders. Many Roman roads still traverse the country, and the Fosse Way, Ermine Street and Akeman Street, which pass through Cirencester, remain in use today. The Corinium Museum gives visitors a taste of what life was like in Roman Britain through life-size reconstructions of a Roman dining room and kitchen. It houses a large collection of fascinating artifacts and archaeological findings including rare mosaics. The remains of the Roman amphitheater stand on nearby Quern Hill. The extraordinary fourteenth-century Church of St. John the Baptist dominates the market square. The impressive south porch was built in 1490, and the brasses in the Trinity Chapel serve as memorials to local wool merchants. A gilt cup made for Henry VIII's Queen Anne Boleyn in 1535 holds a place of honor in the church. There are architecturally striking buildings and beautiful shops on the main streets including the houses of medieval wool merchants and weavers' cottages that stand in Coxwell Street.

The Duntisbournes, about seven miles southwest of Chedworth, are four picturesque stops—all within a few miles of each other—along the stream named for Dunt, a Saxon chief. Duntisbourne Rouse is the site of St. Michael's Church, accessed by a tiny gate set in a tall hedgerow that almost shelters the church from view. Its simple Saxon lines have been embellished by Norman additions. The crypt chapel occupies the space below the Norman chancel and can only be reached by an external staircase. A standing cross with a disfigured head stands in the fourteenth-century churchyard where pathways cross the mossy grass. Neighboring cottages angle toward the old churchyard walls. The road winds on through Middle Duntisbourne and Duntisbourne Leer. Water runs freely through the ford and across the roadway where old cart wheels were once soaked and horses hooves cleaned. Duntisbourne Abbots, the largest of the villages, overhangs the quiet valley. A double gate painted a soft green contrasts with the emerald yews that border the path to the Church of St. Peter. Narrow lanes link the cottages and houses to the churchyard and the villages below.

Barnsley House, located approximately ten miles southeast of Chedworth, is a lovely Queen Anne house known for its exceptional gardens. Famous for her horticulture books, Rosemary Verey has combined the essence of many gardening styles in her small, but magnificent three-acre enclosure. There is a gothic summerhouse, ornamental sculptures, an herb area, a knot garden, fruit trees and beautiful views across the surrounding countryside.

Bibury, about eight miles southeast of Chedworth, is the home of Arlington Row, a remarkable collection of seventeenth-century weavers' cottages. The small houses stand near Rack Isle. Bordered on three sides by water, this small spit of land is where wool was hung out on racks for drying. The roadway follows the River Coln and diminutive footbridges cross the river to access the water meadows. A trout farm and working corn mill display agricultural tools and machinery. The Saxon Church of St. Mary stands at the north end of the village.

The Eastleachs *(See Chapter 2)*

Northleach *(See Chapter 3)*

Wiltshire

Chapter Seven

Castle Combe

To Market

Village buildings and landmarks impart a personal and professional architectural history of local life as it unfolds through the ages. Cottages stand next to shops which look across to an elderly oak tree near the village green or mottled grave stones in a silent churchyard. A private residence might be called The Bakehouse or The Maltings, paying tribute to the trade that once took place on the premises.

As villages grew out of ancient settlements and populations expanded, the age-old practice of buying, selling and trading took on a more formalized role in society. Many of today's marketplaces can trace their humble beginnings to a crossroads or a preferred meeting point near the village center where locals gathered to barter or sell their goods. These early commercial sites were often marked with a cross. The traditional market cross, which can be seen throughout the country, claimed its place in English history.

One of the most revered Christian symbols, crosses stood as reminders that fairness must be an integral element of every transaction. In those times, men would often make an agreement within sight of a church, which to them was the same as in the sight of God.

From the time the Normans arrived in England in 1066, there is verification of charters being issued to hold markets and fairs. A lord of the manor, religious foundation such as a monastery, abbey or nunnery, or officials of a town received a charter from the crown granting the right to hold a weekly market on a designated day in a certain place. A more elaborate fair was usually an annual event. It might run for several days and was held on the feast day of a saint, at a particular location.

Duties were charged on goods sold at these markets and fairs. As it brought significant revenue to the holder, a charter was very valuable. Many communities thrived or failed to survive based on their income from trade.

On market day, traders walked great distances to bring their wares to the market cross. In larger areas, multiple crosses marked locations where selected items could be found. Those selling butter, eggs and produce stood around the butter cross. Corn was traded at the corn cross, herbs and spices at the sage cross, and livestock at the sheep cross. Stalls crowded the narrow streets. In smaller villages, everyone gathered in the same place. In the shadow of their market cross, they hawked their goods while buyers inspected merchandise and argued for a fair price.

As trade routes expanded, goods from the Continent were sold at markets and fairs. Monks would take the opportunity to preach to people who gathered to transact business. On fair days, traveling troupes provided entertainment. Games were played and competitions were organized with great enthusiasm. These events were a welcome break in routine, a chance to socialize, and a brief glimpse of the tastes, sights and sounds that were part of life beyond a rural family's fields and farms.

The design of a market cross is as unique as the village in which it stands. They may be very grand—embellished with statues, intricately carved designs and capped with long, slender top pieces. Some stand alone or are protected by a roof balanced on wood or stone posts. Often the roofs are shingled. Occasionally they are domed or formed in unique shapes. Some have gracefully arched openings between molded and classically trimmed pillars. Others retain a simple cruciform shape set on a solid platform base. In later centuries, a second floor was sometimes added and the market cross became a market house. Ground floors remained open, but upper levels were enclosed and used as town halls, meeting places or guildhalls.

At the time of the Reformation, many crosses were mutilated or demolished. Interestingly, the structures that eventually took their places were still referred to as market crosses.

Modern construction and expanding roadways have frequently displaced these venerable landmarks, but many have been preserved or rebuilt and remain an important thread in the fabric of their villages. They represent long-standing charters and continue to stand witness to contemporary commerce and the daily comings and goings of the modern villages around them.

Castle Combe Today

Castle Combe's handsome market cross stands solidly at the heart of the village. The old water pump is its companion. The simple structure that surrounds the medieval cross is open-sided with four stone columns supporting a lichen-covered, pyramidal roof. Ornately carved, the cross rises from a pedestal thought to date from the fourteenth century, and its shaft reaches skyward through the weathered roof tiles to form a distinctively ornamented stone spire.

History records that in the summer of 1315, King Edward II granted to Bartholomew de Baddlesmore the right to hold a market at the manor of Castle Combe. A further charter was issued by Henry VI in 1440 allowing a weekly market, and the village was once the site of the most notable annual sheep fair in North Wiltshire. Where local traders once gathered, visitors now orient themselves to their exceptional surroundings. The market cross still serves as a gathering place.

In the days when the village flourished as a busy milling and wool weaving center, the waters of the By Brook flowed fast enough to power mills up and down the valley. Signs of this prosperous history are seen throughout the village.

Arriving in Castle Combe, cars are left at a large parking area above the village. Small, picturesque gardens and historical buildings line the walk to the village center. Stepping down the incline, surrounded by wooded hillsides, there is an eighteenth-century thatched cottage, a small lane leading to the school, and an old Congregational schoolroom which, in its latest incarnation, houses the village museum. Dower House dates from around 1700 and displays the shield of the le Scropes, early lords of the manor. An elegantly fashioned shell crowns the front door. From 1804 until 1992, this residence was home to a succession of village doctors.

The White Hart pub stands at the point where the road begins to widen at the market cross. Ale has been served on this site for half a century. A cozy hearth room window looks out on the market cross and the hub of the village. On the other side of the cross is the Castle Hotel. Once a hostelry for monks traveling to Malmesbury Abbey, it was known in pilgrimage times as The Salutation at the Cross.

Down a short pathway is the parish Church of St. Andrew, which dates from the thirteenth century with additions in the century that followed. So many people were buried almost beneath its walls that extensive restoration and stabilization had to be carried out in the middle of the nineteenth century.

The monument to Walter de Dunstanville, great, great grandson of King Henry I and baron of Castle Combe, is an interesting study in symbolism applied to tombs and effigies. His name and date of death, 1270, are engraved across the simple canopy that frames his final resting place which is set into the church wall. The effigy of Sir Walter wears a suit of chain mail. (The way the links are carved identifies the sculptor as a craftsman from Bristol.) His legs are crossed at the knees indicating he went on two crusades. The feet resting on the back of a lion and his hand placed on a drawn sword signify he lost his life in battle. Carved on the base are six "weepers" who mourn his death. It is believed the figures represent the six de Dunstanville children.

Inside the south door is a fifteenth-century font with an unusual stone shelf for the priest's book. The treasured clock without a face stands at the tower base. People would tell time by listening to its chimes. On the exterior of the tower is a relief of weavers' tools—shuttle, shears and comb—that dates from the time of Elizabeth I.

Further down the street is Old Court House, a substantial half-timbered building, and several weavers' cottages where spinning and weaving took place during the village's heyday. When Sir John Fastolf (acknowledged as the man on whom Shakespeare based his Henry VI character

Falstaff) was lord of the manor in the opening years of the fifteenth century, the thirteen mills operating on the By Brook made the clothiers very wealthy. The red and white cloth they created was simply called castlecombe. There is a much-repeated fable about two brothers who were weavers. To combat the cold, they wove large, heavy cloths to wrap themselves in while they slept and gave the covers their own name—Blanket.

A triple arched town bridge over the By Brook was originally built of wood, later replaced by stone. The nearby Manor House Hotel stands on the site of the original fourteenth-century manor hall. When most of the village buildings and properties were sold at auction in 1947, the manor house was converted to a country club with accommodations and is now an elegant, luxury hotel.

Castle Combe has often been used in films and television productions and gracefully maintains its centuries-old appearance. There are no glaring street lights, aerials or overhead wires to mar its pristine beauty. Galleries and shops hide their contemporary ways behind cottage walls. Like the old church and centerpiece market cross, the entire village is arrayed in yellow-gold stone that basks in the scenic abundance of the By Brook and lush hillsides that encircle the village.

Finding Your Way

Castle Combe is about six miles northwest of Chippenham, just off the B4039. The village is signposted.

Nearby Places of Interest

Maud Heath's Causeway, about nine miles southeast of Castle Combe, is a walkway that runs from Wick Hill, near Bremhill, to the market town of Chippenham, a distance of almost five miles. In 1474, the widow of John Hethe, Matilda Hethe—now known as Maud Heath—deeded land and property to a group of trustees for the building and maintenance of a causeway. Since the roadway crossed the River Avon, the track was muddy and the surrounding land flooded frequently. Maud's causeway was raised above ground level by a series of arches, and the bridge that spanned the Avon made it possible for local people to travel to market avoiding the perils of the once hazardous journey through treacherous swampland. A statue of Maud Heath stands in the field at the top of Wick Hill. Though it isn't likely she was a market woman, early accounts regarded her as such and she sits, hands on knees, basket at her side, looking out over the valley. A memorial pillar stands near the river at Kellaways with an inscription that gives a brief account of Maud's bequest. This gift, bestowed in her lifetime, covered the original construction and, through the meticulous accounting and investment practices of the trustees, still provides funds for the causeway's maintenance today, more than five hundred years later.

Biddestone, about three miles southeast of Castle Combe, has a picture postcard look to its small village green. Ducks paddle across the water where cottage lawns flirt with stone boulders and creeping groundcover that form the bank of the pond. Impressive buff-colored buildings and a pub stand close to the curving main thoroughfare as it winds towards the Church of St. Nicholas with its thirteenth-century tower and tree-shaded churchyard.

∾   ∾   ∾

Lacock *(See Chapter 9)*

Chapter Eight

Stourton

An
English Garden

A journey across England is like strolling through the world's most enchanting garden. British gardeners strive to make the earth beautiful by glorifying small and grand spaces alike. They have ways of mixing native species with showy blossoms and clamoring vines that can turn a simple corner into a showplace. Planting trees for shade, cultivating roses for their extravagant blooms, massing walls of shrubbery for privacy—the English garden is immediately recognizable.

Poets and authors are moved by their striking beauty and peaceful settings. Library shelves overflow with volumes on how the green-thumbed English "organize" their gardens into riots of bright color or subdued borders of leafy plants and contrasting textures. From simple cottage entries where climbing wisteria gracefully frame the front door, to elaborate manor houses flanked with lofty trees shading formal terraces, gardening is an art form that has been successfully practiced here for centuries.

Surprisingly, flowers were conspicuously absent from early English gardens. There were practical kitchen gardens marked with rows of vegetables, and herb gardens for cooking and medicinal cuttings, but gardens of pleasure were patterned on formal landscapes of the Continent with symmetrical box hedges, espaliered fruit trees, gravel walkways and impressive fountains.

In the mid-eighteenth century, wealthy owners of English country estates began to rework their immediate surroundings into more natural landscapes that flowed seamlessly into the vast acreage beyond the main house. Rivers were diverted so lakes and ponds could be built. Lacy waterfalls and boulder-strewn streams incorporated the sights and sounds of moving water into the scenery. Great tracts of forested land were cleared to provide broad, uninterrupted vistas. This was gardening on a grand scale, and one of the most ambitious of these creations was the spectacular transformation of Wiltshire's jewel, Stourhead.

Henry Hoare II inherited the massive mansion and grounds from his father in 1741. The Palladian style house incorporated the designs of sixteenth-century Italian architect Andrea Palladio who based his concepts on the buildings of ancient Rome.

Well-versed in the classics, Hoare had a great appreciation for the symbolism classical structures represented in literature as well as art. He had just completed a tour of the Continent where he was particularly impressed with the paintings of Claude Lorrain. They depicted classic architecture set in stunning landscapes and are said to have inspired the layout of the gardens and the placement of the temples, bridges and buildings around Stourhead's breathtaking, man-made lake.

Hoare engaged Henry Flitcroft to work with him on the colossal project. Early in his career, Flitcroft was a draftsman for Richard Boyle, Lord Burlington, a great patron of the arts who promoted the revival of classic architecture in eighteenth-century England. Flitcroft's work was modeled on the designs of Inigo Jones and Andrea Palladio. His ideas were well-suited to the vision Hoare had for Stourhead.

The garden would cover one hundred acres of the 2,650 acre estate—a monumental undertaking. The pristine lake was created by damming the headwaters of the River

Stour. Walking paths were carved through the heavily forested land between the house and lake. The main pathway was continued along the shore near the newly constructed Temple of Flora. Silent sculptures inhabited the flooded grottoes. Its graceful dome silhouetted against greenery, the Pantheon provided a remarkable view across the lake back toward the village.

Further on, a cascading waterfall was created near the rock arch and a narrow corridor passed through a wooded area to the secluded Temple of Apollo. The final curve of the trail looped behind the exquisite arched bridge near the fourteenth-century High Cross that once stood at the crossroads in medieval Bristol. Work on the garden was completed around 1780—almost forty years after it first began.

Native plants populated the original landscape at Stourhead. Later generations of the family added species popular in their lifetimes. Majestic conifers came from North America. The celebrated rhododendrons were a late-eighteenth-century addition, augmented with newly developed varieties in the twentieth century.

The color spectrum within Stourhead's sylvan acres is nothing short of magnificent. Delicate, springtime petals stand out against the evergreens' rich emerald tones. As the weather warms, rhododendrons blush. Even the persistent English mist adds watery-gray brush strokes, softening the bolder hues of leaves and blossoms. As in all gardens, the skill of the caregivers is seen in the introduction of new plants that blend with the surroundings in perfect harmony—a work in progress with infinite potential. Each leaf and every blossom make Henry Hoare II's masterpiece one of the finest of all English gardens.

<u>Stourton Today</u>

Every season takes a turn decorating the quaint village with promising buds, fragrant flowers, changing leaves and bare-branched winter beauty. Nestled near the lake, the village is part of the estate and takes its name from the Stourtons who owned the land before the Hoare family purchased it. The main street descends from the gates of Stourhead House. It passes the Spread Eagle Inn, a walled courtyard of shops, the medieval church dedicated to St. Peter, and a row of charming stone cottages presently used as estate offices, as it makes its way toward the Bristol Cross and the edge of the lake.

Stourhead House was designed and built in 1721 for the first Henry Hoare by Colen Campbell, a renowned neo-classical architect. Henry Hoare II added paintings and sculpture to the family's art collection, but his primary concentration was the development of the now world-famous garden.

When distinguished scholar and historian Richard Colt Hoare inherited the house in 1785, he enlarged the structure by placing a wing on each side of the mansion to house a library and gallery. The house contains exceptional furniture by Thomas Chippendale the younger. In 1902, the central section of the house was almost entirely destroyed by fire, but rebuilt and refurbished according to original specifications. Colt Hoare's Regency additions were not damaged. The sixth Baronet, Henry Hugh Arthur Hoare, having no direct heir, passed the estate to the National Trust in 1947.

The village buildings begin at the Spread Eagle Inn where a familiar name is scratched on one of the windows in the barroom. During World War II, a certain officer was involved in frequent missions to occupied France. His wife, a young mother of two, came down from London to join her husband for a war-time, reunion weekend. Following a popular romantic tradition, they used her diamond ring to sign their names on the glass: David Niven, Primula Niven—1941.

An inn has occupied this location since the eighteenth century. With its Flemish brickwork façade and stone eagle-capped gate pillars, the building retains much of the charm of its early years. On a brisk afternoon, a friendly welcome and two handsome fireplaces help chase away the chill. Food is served in the formal dining room and in the more relaxed atmosphere of the bar. The vaulted beer and wine cellars are still in use, and five beautifully appointed bedrooms are available for those who want to extend their stay.

The parish church of St. Peter has imposing interior stone archwork and numerous monuments to members of the Stourton and Hoare families. Richard Colt Hoare's impressive marble tomb stands on the sloping lawn near the old church. Weatherworn benches invite visitors to stop a while and take pleasure in the serenity of the peaceful churchyard. From this vantage point, there is a dramatic perspective of the Bristol Cross, the graceful Palladian bridge and the Pantheon across the lake.

The centerpiece of the estate is the garden with its serene islands, magnificent classical temples and grottoes. A walkway guides visitors from the house down to the lake. An alternative route follows the main street through the village joining the Eighteenth Century Garden Walk near the Bristol Cross. The distance around the lake is about two miles. Many special events are held throughout the year: sunrise strolls with the head gardener, Shakespeare performed on the terraced lawns, painting sessions at the water's edge and Christmas music followed by traditional mulled wine and mince pies at Stourhead House.

For more than two hundred years, the temples have kept their secrets and the lake has reflected the living landscape. The world may turn faster these days, but Stourhead remains blissfully sheltered in its creator's eighteenth-century vision of beauty and tranquility.

Finding Your Way

Stourton is approximately eight miles south of Frome on the B3092.

Nearby Places of Interest

King Alfred's Tower, just over a mile west of Stourton, is a brick folly built by Henry Flitcroft in the latter part of the eighteenth century. The occasional narrow windows in the outer walls provide light for the well-worn set of more than 200 steps rising 160 feet to the observation area at the top of the tower. There are seemingly endless views across Wiltshire and the neighboring counties of Dorset and Somerset. In the summer of 1944, a plane with five American servicemen aboard crashed into the fog-shrouded tower. Lighter shades of brick show where it was repaired in the 1960s. The tower is built on the site where King Alfred assembled his forces to turn back a ninth-century attack by invading Danes.

Longleat House, about nine miles northeast of Stourton, was built in 1580. All the major rooms are positioned to look out on the splendid landscape surrounding the grand Elizabethan house. It is the current home of Alexander Thynn, the seventh Marquess of Bath. Seven libraries at Longleat house more than forty thousand volumes, five thousand of which are in the famous Red Library. The state dining room, drawing room and Prince of Wales bedroom are only a few of the gilded, richly decorated rooms open to the public. Capability Brown designed the Half Mile Pond and other garden features in the mid-eighteenth century. Today, Longleat boasts a drive-through safari experience with lowland gorillas, hippos, elephants and other exotic residents roaming divided sections of the estate. There are five cleverly designed mazes to baffle visitors, including the world's longest hedge maze, and a variety of other sights and activities like the narrow-gauge railway and butterfly garden.

Chapter Nine

Lacock

Worth a
Thousand Words

Photos are like history books in miniature. They record exactly how things appear at precise seconds in time. The first photographs were nothing short of small miracles achieved by mixing various amounts of chemicals and testing light and time. The images were elusive, fast-fading. How to capture and retain these visual representations challenged the mind and imagination. The photographic phenomenon was destined to bring the greater world closer to home. Patience, artistry and new techniques were required. A number of talented individuals, experimenting independently, contributed to the discovery and development of the art and science of photography.

William Henry Fox Talbot, one of these pioneers, was born in England in 1800. His father, William Talbot of Lacock Abbey, was a commissioned army officer who died when his son was only five months old. Fox Talbot spent his early years with his mother and stepfather in the homes of relatives or traveling through England and Europe. He excelled in school, mastering languages and exploring mathematics and science. Graduating from Trinity College, Cambridge, he continued to pursue a life-long interest in botany, astronomical and optical sciences and often met with noted scientists while traveling on the Continent.

In 1827, the family took up residence at Lacock Abbey. His notebooks are filled with extensive entries on the varied scientific experiments he carried out at his permanent home base. During these years, he became increasingly focused on the intricacies of optics and the phenomenon of perception of vision.

While in Italy, Fox Talbot used a camera lucida in an attempt to sketch the beauty of the superb Lake Como scenery. The device allowed an artist to look through a lens which contained a reflecting prism. Seeing a faint image on the paper, the artist could then fill in the outline. However, this method required drawing skills which Fox Talbot simply did not have.

He then tried using the camera obscura to capture the view, but the scene was only temporarily reflected on paper and not imprinted in a lasting way. His scientific mind was intrigued by the notion of transferring a natural image to paper where it would remain as a permanent record.

Fox Talbot began a series of experiments using a common salt solution followed by a silver nitrate solution to sensitize paper. In the summer of 1835, he produced what he called a photogenic drawing of the oriel window in the south gallery of Lacock Abbey. He had created a paper negative from which multiple prints could be made.

At the same time, Louis Jacques Mande Daguerre, a French scene painter, was producing permanent images employing a silver-coated metal plate. His innovation was made public, and Fox Talbot decided to present his own findings to the Royal Society within a few weeks of Daguerre's announcement.

The work intensified. Fox Talbot refined the sensitivity of his method and called the process Calotype—incorporating "kalos" which means beautiful in Greek. With extended exposure times, only static objects could be used as subjects. When exposure times were significantly reduced, portraiture became possible. Fox Talbot took The Footman—the earliest image of a person on paper—in October 1840. It depicts a carriage with the door held open by a footman. His dark knee breeches and waistcoat are trimmed in a contrasting fabric. The cutaway jacket is light colored and the brim of his tall, top hat casts a slight shadow across his face as he looks into the camera.

A studio and printing works was opened a few years later which produced Fox Talbot's *Pencil of Nature*, a description of his research. Illustrated with photos like "The Haystack," which showed rich texture and detail, it was the first publication produced for sale that featured photo illustrations.

In later life, Fox Talbot continued to experiment with photographic reproduction and devoted his life to scholarly learning. One of his most notable achievements was the complicated translations of Assyrian Cuneiform.

William Henry Fox Talbot died at Lacock in 1877. His work in mathematics, physics, astronomy and botany were valued in his lifetime, and history honors his name for the intellectual contributions he made to the scientific advancement of society.

Lacock Today

Lacock provides photo opportunities around every corner. Visitors can follow in the footsteps of William Henry Fox Talbot eyeing similar images and vistas he captured in his nineteenth-century Calotypes.

The focal point of the landscape is the magnificent abbey founded by Ela, Countess of Salisbury in 1232. It stands in an airy meadow that was part of her original manor. She dedicated the abbey to the memory of her husband and served as the first abbess. A door beneath the window that appears in Fox Talbot's famous negative opens onto the Cloister Court. The stone within iron railings memorializes Ela.

At the time of Henry the VIII's Dissolution of the Monasteries, the property was purchased by William Sharington who destroyed the church and made the abbey his private home. The southeast tower (with the exception of the top room) and the stable courtyard additions are open to view. His ornate chimneys are a striking sixteenth-century feature.

Sharington's brother Henry succeeded him. His daughter, Olive, married John Talbot, a descendent of Ela, and the first Talbot came to Lacock.

The story goes that the family was not in favor of the match. The young woman threw herself from the tower to be with her true love waiting below. Olive's father agreed that if she was willing to go to such great lengths, the two should be married.

Changes made by successive generations of the family can be seen in and around the abbey, including a small botanic garden and the catalpa, tulip and grand plane trees planted by Fox Talbot. The grounds are especially lovely in spring when jaunty snowdrop blossoms cover the lawns.

In 1946, Matilda Theresa Talbot presented the Lacock Abbey Magna Carta, one of the family's most prized treasures, to the British Museum. This final form of the Magna

Carta was reissued by Henry III in 1225 and is thought to have found its way to Lacock among the personal papers of Ela, Countess of Salisbury. The museum made two copies: One is on display in the Stone Gallery of the abbey, and the other resides in the Library of Congress in Washington, D.C.

The Fox Talbot Museum is housed in a medieval barn near the entrance to the abbey. It commemorates his work and displays early equipment used in developing his photographic methods.

Turning into East Street, there is a massive fourteenth-century tithe barn. It has a dirt floor, extensive cruck framework and eight bays built to hold the rents—crops and fleece, among other commodities—paid to the abbey.

There was an early Saxon place of worship on the site of St. Cyriac's Church, but the present church dates largely from the fifteenth century. Its graceful spire was added in the seventeenth century. The Lady Chapel, to the left of the altar, is the burial site of several members of the Sharington and Talbot families. The lords and ladies of Lackham, an estate adjacent to Lacock, are memorialized in the south transept. Embedded in the floor is the Baynard brass, which commemorates Robert, his wife Elizabeth, and their thirteen sons and five daughters. It is dated 1501. Fox Talbot's grave can be found in a small cemetery on the opposite edge of the village.

The Bide Brook parallels Church Street. An early eighteenth-century packhorse bridge arches over the stream. Walkers can zigzag through the kissing gate and cross the neighboring fields to experience more of Lacock's picturesque surroundings.

A variety of shops, pubs and bed and breakfast establishments cluster together to form the heart of the village, but perhaps the most intriguing is the fifteenth-century Sign of the Angel. The inn takes its name from an old gold coin called an angel. Its steep, tiled roofs protect the half-timbered upper stories and medieval foundation stones. The entry from the street opens into a wide passage once used to take horses through to the rear yard. The back area is now a casual arrangement of tables and chairs, contrasting nicely with the richly polished antiques, candlelight and fresh flowers of the enchanting, low-ceilinged dining room and creaking stairs leading to the upper bedrooms.

The George Inn dates from 1361 and has a rare dog wheel. Small-stature dogs, turnspits, were bred to run inside the wheel set at eye level in the wall. The wheel was connected to a spit in the large fireplace around the corner. As the dog ran, the spit revolved, and the food cooked over the open flame. The log that forms the inset piece at the top of the fireplace is from a twelfth-century tree limb.

The venerable abbey watches over the village, a spectator to centuries of change. Lacock's half-timbered Tudor buildings, sturdy stone cottages, and fine Georgian-style houses leave a lasting impression of quiet beauty and a clear invitation to return.

Finding Your Way

Lacock is approximately three miles south of Chippenham, just off the A350.

<u>Nearby Places of Interest</u>

Bradford-on-Avon, about nine miles southwest of Lacock, boasts a wonderful, medieval bridge across the River Avon with a lovely domed structure perched on the end. The small building, carved in mellow grey stone, originally served as a wayfarers' chapel. In the sixteenth century, it was converted to a two-prisoner lockup. The town is filled with interesting buildings related to the days when Bradford thrived as a prosperous wool center including the seventeenth-century homes of Dutch weavers. Its notable fourteenth-century tithe barn is more than 167 feet long. The oak doors are studded with original nail work. The Shambles, Market Street and Silver Street are the main shopping thoroughfares. The diminutive Saxon Church of St. Laurence, built around 700 A.D., was rediscovered after serving many different uses. It was restored in the late nineteenth century.

Corsham Court, located about three miles northwest of Lacock, has an impressive collection of paintings and statues by Italian and Flemish masters including Caravaggio, Lipi, Rubens and Van Dyck. The Sleeping Cupid by Michelangelo, one of the great treasures of the Methuen collection, dates from 1496. The gardens were designed by Capability Brown. His almost hidden Gothic Bath House stands in the grounds near the lake completed by Humphrey Repton from Brown's original plan.

Bowood, about five miles northeast of Lacock, was purchased by the first Earl of Shelburne in 1754. The magnificent parklands were designed by Capability Brown. Visitors enter the house through the Orangery built by Robert Adam where the Landsdowne collection of sculpture and paintings, including a number of family portraits, is displayed. The early-nineteenth-century chapel is still used today. The laboratory, a small chamber near the library, is where oxygen was discovered by Joseph Priestley in 1774. Several exhibition rooms display fine porcelain, exquisite jewelry, textiles and furniture including Queen Victoria's wedding chair. There are watercolors by Turner, and Napoleon's death mask is part of the exceptional Bowood Napoleonic Collection. During the rhododendron flowering season, visitors can stroll along two miles of pathways through a sixty-acre woodland garden of lush rhododendrons and blossoming azaleas.

Castle Combe *(See Chapter 7)*
Avebury *(See Chapter 11)*

Chapter Ten

Great Wishford

The
Oak Apple Tradition

How many times had she taken this path through the forest? Though Sarah didn't really understand the ancient rights her parents talked about, she knew Grovely Woods was a special place. The freedom to enter the forest lands had to be protected—reclaimed each year by a contingent of Great Wishford villagers just as their ancestors had done before them.

Spring rain glistened on the oak leaves. Acorns crunched beneath her feet. The great trees towered over her, at times blocking out the sky with their heavy canopies. Sarah took up a branch to use as a walking stick. It was a sturdy bough that reached well past her shoulder. She liked the feel of the rough wood in her small hand.

As she walked along, the only sounds she heard were the same ones that had kept the mighty oaks company here for hundreds of years. It wouldn't be so still in the wood tomorrow.

The moonlight moved softly, playfully dodging the clouds to illuminate the gardens below. Sarah rolled on her side, waking from her springtime dream. She crawled from her bed and struggled to push open the casement. It was the middle of the night, but leaning out, she could see the lanterns and torch lights profiling the crowd of villagers as they marched down the hill.

Some banged on drums, others laid large, wooden ladles against iron pots and old tin buckets. There was even a bugler! Everyone shouted at the same time: "Grovely, Grovely, Grovely, and all Grovely."

She could hear her mother and father at the front door calling out to the revelers. Sarah smiled. It was May 29, Oak Apple Day. The festivities had begun.

Dressing quickly, she raced down the stairs and out into the yard. The chanting grew louder as the throng approached their gate.

The duty of waking the village on Oak Apple Day belonged to the young people of Great Wishford, and they took their job seriously. Clattering along, singing and shouting, it was clear that no one in the vicinity would sleep any more this night.

As the first light of dawn colored the rooftops, Sarah and her family joined their relatives and neighbors to walk the few miles to Grovely Woods. Some pulled small carts; others held hands or linked arms as they strolled up the winding lane. Light spilled from the windows and doorways of the houses they passed. A large group gathered in front of the Royal Oak Inn, and the chant was taken up again as they approached the wood.

Forest rights had been enjoyed by the villagers since the twelfth century. Lords, freeholders and tenants of the manor were permitted to gather dead and fallen branches from the wood throughout the year.

They could cut and take away green boughs only during the month of May. These rights would continue to be honored as long as village representatives annually renewed their claim before the high altar of Salisbury Cathedral.

A Forest Charter, revised in 1603, verified these important rights and clearly stated which part of Grovely Woods could be accessed for the collecting of wood. In times past, residents of Barford St. Martin also held forest rights, but they had to stay on their side of the wood. Folks from Great Wishford could wander "all Grovely."

The villagers marched into the woodlands to exercise their May rights and set about trimming branches from the massive oaks. By tradition, a cut limb could not exceed the girth of a man's forearm.

Small as she was, Sarah could barely see over the stack of kindling she juggled in front of her. Soft, rounded lumps remained attached to some of the sticks. These were the oak apples—nests of gall wasps—from which the celebration took its name. Her mother held a sizeable, antler-shaped branch perfect for mounting over their front door to commemorate the day. By mid-morning, every village house would be decorated in woodsy splendor.

Sarah watched several men heft a large piece of timber destined to trim the highest point of St. Giles Church. This was the marriage bough. Festooned in brightly colored ribbons, it would be placed near the top of the tower as a symbol of luck to the couples who married in the church during the next twelve months.

To secure the forest rights for the coming year, a group of villagers traveled the half-dozen miles to the west door of Salisbury Cathedral. Clad in costumes reflecting the style of the early 1800s, four women performed two time-honored dances: one with bundles of dry wood, one using oak twigs.

Then the terms of the Forest Charter were read for all to hear. With a resounding shout of the required words, "Grovely, Grovely, Grovely, and all Grovely," the villagers reaffirmed their claim.

The merriment continued throughout the day. When it was time to name the May Queen, Sarah happily joined in the celebration. She walked in procession through the village streets past the post office, around the old churchyard wall to the River Wylye bridge that marked the boundary of the parish. As the entourage turned back to re-enter the village, some remained on the bridge waving their treasured oak branches as tradition dictated.

The childhood commemorations of Oak Apple Day remained a special memory for Sarah just as they did for the other young people of the village. In later years, they would preserve the traditions and keep the ancient customs alive for Great Wishford … all of Great Wishford.

Great Wishford Today

The main road to the village crosses over the stone bridge that spans the River Wylye. Waving reeds shelter sleek mallards as they silently paddle near the grassy banks keeping their eyes on the swift-moving current.

St. Giles Church stands at the head of the village, surrounded by a low, stone wall. The famous breadstones, set into the northeast corner of the exterior of the wall, record the price of loaves beginning with the year 1800. At the turn of the nineteenth century, a French blockade severely limited the importing of wheat. The price of bread soared and was particularly high in Great Wishford. It was common practice in those days for a baker to post the price, written in stone, in the local churchyard. The cost is listed per gallons, based on the dry volume of the ingredients. A gallon equaled four two-pound loaves.

The Wishford breadstones are unique in that stones from later years were preserved to form a permanent, historic collection. The original, worn tablets were copied and replaced during the last century. The stones for the war years stand out among the others because of their notations: 1920 "after the great war," and 1946–1948 "bread rationed—subsidized price." In 2000, the parish council added a millennium engraving to denote the two hundredth anniversary of the stones. The price on the first stone is 3s 4d (three shillings, four pence) per gallon. The latest price is £3.72p (three pounds, seventy-two pence).

Tall, dignified yew trees flank the pebble path that leads to the church. The wrought iron porch gate is adorned with gold stars and behind it, a heavy wooden door opens to reveal the interior of the church.

In the north aisle, there is a monument to Nicholas de Bonham, an early lord of the manor who died in 1386. Covered by a protective mat on the floor nearby are the commemorative brasses of Thomas Bonham, Edith Bonham and their nine children, seven of whom were said to have been septuplets. At the east end of the chancel is the Grobham memorial. Sir Richard was lord when the 1603 Forest Charter was rewritten. History records that he killed the last wild boar in England. Curiously, the villagers have chosen their church as the venue for displaying an early parish fire engine. Made of wood, it was purchased in 1728, and the original operating instructions remain with it.

Narrow, angled streets wind around the churchyard. The almshouses, endowed by the Grobhams, face the church. Close by is Great Wishford School. Built in 1722, its bricks are set in a distinctive checkered pattern. Further up the hill, houses made of Chilmark stone stand close to the road that leads to the Royal Oak Inn and Grovely Woods.

On May 29, today's residents confirm their ancient rights in the age-old way followed by a day-long celebration in Oak Apple Field near the center of the village. Costumes, competitions, children circling the May Pole—it's a time for remembering the past and looking forward to the coming year.

Finding Your Way

Great Wishford is about six miles northwest of Salisbury. Follow the A36 in the direction of Wilton. Continue on the A36 approximately three miles to the village turnoff which is signposted.

Nearby Places of Interest

Salisbury, located about six miles southeast of Great Wishford, was granted a charter in 1227. It sits proudly where the Rivers Avon and Nadder come together. A showplace of winding medieval streets, Salisbury glories in its six-hundred-year-old poultry market, merchants' halls, historic inns, and whitewashed, half-timbered houses. The eighteenth-century guildhall looks over the market square. Since the mid-fourteenth-century, markets have been held here twice each week. The 404-foot tower of the city's magnificent cathedral is the tallest spire in England. It was added at a later date to the architecturally interesting flying buttresses and gothic arches of the magnificent cathedral structure completed in the mid-thirteenth century. Among the tombs and memorials, a fourteenth-century clock, the oldest in England, is located in the north aisle. An original copy of the Magna Carta resides in the Chapter House. Surrounding the cathedral precincts is the Close with its four gateways. Several Georgian-styled houses and gardens stand within the Close. The Salisbury and South Wiltshire Museum contains informative displays on Stonehenge and Old Sarum, and The Wardrobe exhibits regimental gear and military trappings. In the care of the National Trust, beautiful Mompesson House was built in 1701 for Charles Mompesson, a local Member of Parliament. It has a grand staircase with elaborate plasterwork and is furnished as a Georgian gentleman's residence.

∾ ∾ ∾

Old Sarum's fortifications, just north of Salisbury, are covered-over with grass. When construction began on the cathedral, the population gathered near the new church and the hilltop town, once home to Celts, Romans, Saxons and Normans, was deserted. Today, only the stone foundations remain of the ancient settlement that once dominated the surrounding plain.

∾ ∾ ∾

Wilton House, approximately three miles south of Great Wishford, started life as a ninth-century nunnery that was replaced by a twelfth-century abbey. The building and surrounding property were given to William Herbert by Henry VIII at the time of the Dissolution of the Monasteries. It has continued to be the home of the Earls of Pembroke, who also own a large part of Great Wishford village and the adjacent lands, since that time. The Double Cube room is one of the house's most fascinating features. The room has perfectly equal dimensions: 60 feet long by 30 feet wide by 30 feet high. An eighteenth-century Palladian bridge spans the River Nadder as it carves its way through Wilton Park.

Teffont Evias, about seven miles west of Wilton, is an engaging village named for Ralph Ewyas who purchased the manor there in the late eleventh century. Its main street shadows the course of a fast-flowing stream where simple footbridges cross the water and enter the quiet gardens of picturesque stone cottages. The Church of St. Michael and All Angels stands near the present manor house. In the north aisle, three distinguished armor-clad figures lay side by side. Henry Ley, who acquired the manor from King Henry VIII, rests besides William and Matthew, two of his six sons. The remaining paint on the striking figures is original. There are also several memorials to the Maynes who acquired the manor in 1692. Descendents of that family are the present owners of the manor.

❧   ❧   ❧

Teffont Magna, a short distance from Teffont Evias, was once a bustling village and busy stop on the stage route. Today, the former smithy, malt house, coaching inn and Methodist chapel are private residences. The village has its own church, St. Edward King of the West Saxons, a simple structure where pieces of a Saxon cross and a thirteenth-century bell are displayed. The lanes of both villages provide delightful walks past charming cottages—many with thatched roofs.

Chapter Eleven

Avebury

Mysterious
Stone Circles

O f the many inspiring sites that adorn the English countryside, the ancient stone circles of Avebury seem to represent an entirely different dimension. It is an uncommon place whose significance remains elusive.

Stepping into the ancient stone circle, larger and older than Stonehenge, visitors move away from the modern world. The reality of the nearby village recedes in favor of the mysterious and unexplained. The sheer magnitude of the massive stone sentinels, whether wrapped in the hush of newly fallen snow, touched by glancing shafts of bright sunshine or eerily emerging from a morning mist, arouses a reaction of quiet amazement.

A prehistoric tribe settled and began to farm the land at nearby Windmill Hill in the fourth millennium B.C. They were the ancestors of the people who built Avebury about two thousand years later. The Avebury site was strategically located at the base of the Marlborough Downs with Windmill Hill to the northwest, the River Kennet to the south and several burial sites within close proximity.

The scene unfolded in circles. A large ring of stones, bordered by an embankment and deep ditch with four entrances, enclosed two smaller stone spheres of approximately the same size. The perimeter circle consisted of an estimated ninety-eight stones; the northern inner circle had twenty-seven and the southern circle twenty-nine.

In 1648, John Aubrey was hunting near Avebury. Examining the abandoned earthworks and massive stones, he made them out to be part of an ancient temple complex. Aubrey also explored Stonehenge and other ancient settings in Britain.

In the following century, Dr. William Stukeley, studying sacred landscape monuments, made detailed surveys of the Avebury site that proved to be valuable records for later archaeologists.

Sarsen stones, from which the circles were made, are exceptionally hard, massive rocks. The sizable stones, scattered across the nearby Marlborough Downs, were thought to have been named for "Saracens" or foreigners because they seem unrelated to the soft, chalk downland that surrounded them.

The sustained effort to move the stones was tremendous. The gigantic boulders would have been placed on a series of wooden rollers and moved by teams of men pulling on heavy, woven ropes. At designated points forming the circles and avenues leading to the circles, shallow openings were dug into the ground to position the stones. Using ropes and timbers to lever each sarsen into a standing position, the workers balanced the stone in its hole and packed rocks around the base to solidify the placement.

The sarsens raised at Stonehenge, less than twenty miles away, were dressed—carefully sculpted into blocks with carved extensions and indentations for fitting them together. The profile of each Avebury stone exhibits a rough and weathered, natural appearance. These sarsens were selected for their tall, elongated or shorter, broad, diamond-shaped qualities. Visually scanning the contours of the standing stones, it has been suggested they represent masculine and feminine shapes. There is a touching symmetry to the arrangement.

As recently as the eighteenth century, the inner circle to the north, which Stukeley called the Cove, had three large sarsens. Only two remain. The larger of the two is estimated to weigh more than sixty tons. The southern inner circle featured a central stone. The Obelisk, which does not survive, was surrounded by a group of stones known as the Z Feature, a few of which are still standing today.

The ditch was originally about thirty feet deep. It was dug using primitive implements like large bones from cattle and pronged antlers. Originally, the walls of the ditch, hewn from the chalk, would have been a striking white.

Impressive ceremonial avenues of evenly spaced stones led away from the circle. West Kennet Avenue, to the south, was edged with pairs of sarsens marking the way (one and one-half miles) from the great circle to a place known as the Sanctuary, site of a double stone ring and earlier wooden structures. Recent evidence supporting Stukeley's claim of the existence of a southwestern avenue, Beckhampton, is currently under renewed archaeological examination.

Centuries after the site was abandoned, there were still farming settlements close by. Saxons followed by the Normans increased the population in the area. In the Middle Ages, several of the stones were toppled and others were buried by people who regarded them as remnants of ancient pagan rites.

Others of the mammoth sarsens were broken up and used as a ready supply of building materials. The ditch was partially filled in, and houses and outbuildings began to appear within the circle.

Alexander Keiller, a wealthy archaeologist, purchased Avebury and undertook extensive excavations of the monument and surrounding sites during the 1930s. He located many of the lost and fallen stones and returned them to their original positions in the circles and along the West Kennet Avenue. Between the existing ancient stones, concrete markers indicate the spots where additional stones would have stood.

The Swindon Stone weighs more than fifty tons and stands at the northern entrance to the circle. The Barber's Stone got its name when efforts to raise the sarsen in 1938 uncovered the skeletal remains of a man believed to have been a fourteenth-century barber-surgeon. Coins dating from the reign of King Edward I, a scissors and lancet-like object were found with the bones. Keiller found the so-called Repaired Stone in the building foundation of what was once a blacksmith's forge.

The purpose of the Avebury stone circles—why they were erected and what meaning they had—is not decisively known. Radiocarbon dating procedures, aerial photography techniques and ongoing archaeological field work continue to uncover important evidence.

The extraordinary World Heritage Site leaves an unforgettable impression. Documented discoveries coupled with dramatic speculation only begin to reconstruct the story of ancient cultures and the impact of the distant past on the present and the future.

Avebury Today

The medieval village of Avebury, with its twenty-first-century touches, grew up among the mystifying stone circles of prehistory. It is a place that combines the secrets of Neolithic builders with the overt arrival of "modern" amenities. A church with Saxon features, an Elizabethan manor house, a sprinkling of thatched cottages and small farms claimed their rightful space as one century followed the next. Modern roadways carve their way through the countryside and cross the precincts of the stone circles by way of the four original openings, converting ancient corridors to rural thoroughfares. A great part of the area is under the protection of the National Trust.

The Church of St. James dates from about the year 1000. Some of the Saxon windows that graced the early church survive. Aisles were added in the twelfth century, made wider in the fifteenth century and now accommodate polished pews with traditional, cross-stitched, blue hassocks on which members of the congregation kneel.

The magnificently restored rood screen survived the Reformation. In the mid-1500s, crosses and rood screens were removed from churches and destroyed. The Avebury rood screen and loft were bravely concealed behind plaster and rediscovered in 1810. The Victorian restoration carefully reproduced the exquisite colors seen today. A tablet on the north wall commemorates Dame Susanna Holford who died in 1722. She provided funds for the founding of a school in Avebury for children whose parents were unable to teach them how to read. The charitable endowment is still maintained today.

Established in 1938, the Alexander Keiller Museum honors the work of archaeologist Keiller who owned Avebury Manor until his death in 1955. Artifacts found by Keiller and other researchers while excavating the ancient sites that make up the Avebury complex are on display. With the help of exhibits and interactive presentations, The Barn Gallery details the history and unique beauty of Avebury as part of the surrounding landscape.

A narrow walkway crosses the lawns to the sedate sixteenth-century manor house of which the east wing is the oldest section. Medieval walls protect the curling topiary and sculpted flowerbeds of the peaceful manor gardens. Across the road, an old stone dovecote shelters among the trees at the rear of the church. Its nesting pigeons once provided the only meat during long winter months.

The Red Lion Inn pub, with its white walls and heavy thatched roof, stands at the intersection of the main roads passing through Avebury. It dates from the early eighteenth century when it served as a coaching inn on the busy London route.

Meandering to the opposite end of the village, the street divides the northeast and southeast sections of the stone circle. The restored United Reform Church, founded in 1670, was built from stones taken from the Avebury site.

A few charming, old buildings cluster near the simple entrance gate to the great embankment. Passing through the opening and into the circle, the impact of the stones is remarkable.

Visitors can walk right up to the sarsens and make their way across the vast enclosure moving between and around the megaliths for a closer look. Information plaques are positioned along the route to tell the story of the stones. The trees and village stand quietly in the background, bringing the ancient and the present together in an oddly harmonious setting.

Finding Your Way

Avebury is about six miles west of Marlborough. Follow the A4 and turn north on the B4003. The site and village are signposted.

Nearby Places of Interest

Windmill Hill, approximately one and one-half miles north of Avebury, is an ancient causeway enclosure. The remnants of the earthworks form three, rough, concentric circles. Knives, flint axes and other household objects, including pieces of pottery now known as Windmill Hill pottery, have been recovered from the site. It has been determined that it was not a place of permanent settlement. Rather, it is thought to have been a meeting place where area tribes came together for ceremonial gatherings or festivals.

∽ ∽ ∽

Silbury Hill, about a mile south of Avebury, stands 130 feet high. It is Europe's largest prehistoric man-made mound. Shaped from chalk and soil, the hill covers more than five acres and was engineered in horizontal terraces and then covered over with earth, leaving the top flat. There are many legends and myths about the site. One is that a king named Sil was buried under the mound. Another told of hidden riches— a rider and a golden horse. It was constructed about the same time as the stone circles at Avebury. Scientific researchers have carbon dated the site to about 2600 B.C. Samples of plant life and remnants of insects indicate construction was underway in late summer. Much excavation work has been carried out at Silbury, but the purpose of the mound remains unknown.

అ   అ   అ

West Kennet Long Barrow, located about one and one-half miles south of Avebury, is a chambered burial mound laid out in the shape of a trapezoid 330 feet long. Massive sarsen stones stand at the entrance and were used to form the interior burial chambers. The long barrow was used for several centuries and then sealed off. In subsequent years, it was reopened and the contents looted. During excavations in the 1950s, the remains of more than forty men, women and children were found in the sealed chambers off the main passage along with several pieces of pottery, jewelry and tools.

అ   అ   అ

Cherhill White Horse, about four and one-half miles west of Avebury, is one of several fascinating horse carvings that appear on the chalk downs of the Wiltshire landscape. It is one of the oldest horse cuttings, dating from 1780. One-hundred-and-forty feet long, the carving is said to have been directed from the hill below while a group of volunteers artistically cut through the turf to expose the white chalk beneath. The prancing figure can be seen from forty miles away. To keep them from standing out as landmarks, the Wiltshire white horses were concealed during World War II.

                                    ❧   ❧   ❧

Castle Combe *(See Chapter 7)*
Lacock *(See Chapter 9)*

Hampshire

Chapter Twelve

Chawton

Revisiting

Jane

Influenced by two very different periods of English history, Jane Austen lived more than half her life in the eighteenth century and the remaining years in the nineteenth, coming to stay at Chawton in 1809. It is considered her literary home.

First Impressions and *Elinor and Marianne*, which would one day bear the memorable titles *Pride and Prejudice* and *Sense and Sensibility,* were written earlier, but Austen spent her first, peaceful years at Chawton revising both manuscripts. During the prolific Chawton years, *Sense and Sensibility* was published in 1811 and *Pride and Prejudice* appeared two years later. She wrote and published *Mansfield Park* in 1814 and completed *Persuasion* in 1816, the same year *Emma* was published. She also recovered *Susan*, later renamed *Northhanger Abbey*, from a publisher who had earlier elected not to release the novel. In addition, she completed the first twelve chapters of *Sanditon*.

For the most part, the traditions and activities of her novels are those she experienced herself. In Austen's day, girls were educated at home or sometimes attended boarding schools. They usually studied a little French, some music, dancing, drawing and perhaps gained practical instruction in sewing and embroidery. She and her sister Cassandra went to school in Oxford, Southampton and Reading, returning home after a few short years. They used their father's fine library to continue their education from that time on.

The social season revolved around grand balls, dancing the quadrille or polka, dinner parties and musical evenings— the "coming out" of young women into society. These were occasions for people to meet and eventually make a marriage match. Days were spent calling on friends and visiting neighbors in and around the district. Young women passed the evening hours at the pianoforte entertaining the family or reading poetry and popular gothic novels. Books were expensive, and lending libraries became popular. The lives of the Austen sisters followed this pattern.

Regency England was ruled by strict convention. Austen used the rigid standards of the time to frame the actions of her characters. Morals, ethics, religion, politics—the drama of daily life according to complex rules sparred with romantic dreams and aspirations, but propriety took precedence.

When a gentleman wanted to meet a young lady, he found someone who knew her to make a formal introduction. The couple was then free to see each other in well-chaperoned circumstances. If a young woman wanted to meet a young man, she waited for him to approach her in the accepted way. For her to approach him would have caused a scandal.

Young women of the time were always accompanied by a brother or older, usually married woman. In the summer months, society shifted their activities to resort areas. A more relaxed way of getting to know someone was for a couple to stroll along the promenade and stop for tea at one of the many public rooms, provided the formal introductions had been carried out first.

Enjoying a holiday in the West Country, Austen herself met a young man and fell in love, but he died before they could make plans for their future. Not long after, she accepted a proposal from a wealthy landowner only to change her mind the very next day.

Austen had a flair for making the ordinary things in life interesting. Her female characters wore layers of soft, white muslin echoing the fashion of the day: empire style dresses with embroidered hems and appliquéd collars. Men dressed in fine coats, waistcoats, trousers, tall hats and carried gloves.

Her country house backgrounds provided a history of period design complemented by innovations of the day. She peopled her stories with vivid personalities, and always took a satirical, humorous look at social pretensions.

Her writing took a serious, productive turn when she was in her early twenties. But when her father retired for health reasons and moved his wife and daughters to Bath, she wrote only sporadically.

Upon Reverend Austen's death, the sisters, with Mrs. Austen, went to live with their brother Frank and his family in Southampton. After Edward, another of the Austen brothers, inherited the Chawton estate, he offered his mother, sisters and their friend Martha Lloyd a modest house there. It wasn't until she returned to the pastoral countryside and made her home in rural Chawton that Austen's creativity flourished once again.

At the age of forty-one, Austen left her beloved Chawton and moved to Winchester to be near her physician. Greatly debilitated by Addison's Disease, a tubercular kidney ailment, she died on July 18, 1817 and is buried in the north aisle of Winchester Cathedral. The following year saw the posthumous publication of *Persuasion* and *Northanger Abbey*.

Chawton Today

The window of Jane Austen's dining room looks directly onto the main street of the village. When the road was a busy thoroughfare, travelers in passing carriages could see the family enjoying a meal, just as today's visitors to the museum glimpse what life was like for the author in the years she made Chawton her home.

The red brick house is filled with Austen's possessions. A display case in the drawing room shows off prized pieces of jewelry, a lock of her hair, other personal items and several important letters. Paper was very costly so correspondents of the day employed a clever inverted, intra-line writing technique. They used the spaces between the written lines to compose a new letter. Recipients, not senders, paid for the delivery of a letter.

On the Clementi piano, similar to the one Austen owned, is one of her music manuscripts. The glass-fronted bookcase originally belonged to her father and holds several first editions of her novels.

The small table where Austen did her writing stands near the window in the dining room. After her daughter's death, Mrs. Austen moved the table to a cottage she had furnished for an elderly servant. When the importance of the table became clear, it was sent back to the family. A letter about the return of the table hangs above it on the wall.

Family portraits and silhouettes decorate the cheerful room. Also displayed are a number of original family letters and a copy of Austen's estate, leaving almost all her money and possessions to her sister. In her second floor bedroom, there is a lace collar made by Austen and other pieces of her needlework. Among the other rooms is a costume gallery showcasing clothing fashionable during the Regency period.

The yard includes a granary, now a lecture room, the old well, the small wood-sided bakehouse, and Austen's donkey carriage. She used it to run errands and was often seen driving along the Chawton-Alton road in the little wooden cart.

Austen's letters contain references to the columbine, lilacs, laburnums and peonies that graced the family's well-loved garden. These plant varieties are still part of the garden today.

Cozy thatched cottages, their fences almost linking one to the other, stand near the Grey Friars pub across from Jane Austen's house. Further along the road is the seventeenth-century manor house Edward Austen inherited from Thomas Knight. Standing in a quiet meadow nearby is the Church of St. Nicholas.

The original structure dated from the thirteenth century. Rebuilt after a ruinous fire, the present church is largely Victorian. It features a few memorials remaining from earlier years. Mrs. Austen and Cassandra are buried in the churchyard.

The popularity of her novels and a recent resurgence of interest in her work as seen in screen adaptations bring huge numbers of visitors to Chawton. They come to see the Jane Austen House museum—a reminder of daily life in a fascinating age and a tribute to the memory of a notable woman writer.

Finding Your Way

Chawton is about a mile south of Alton, just off the A31. The village is signposted.

Nearby Places of Interest

Selborne, approximately three miles southeast of Chawton, has strong associations with the eighteenth-century naturalist Gilbert White. He lived and worked in this lovely village, writing about the area's plant and animal life in *The Natural History of Selborne,* first published in 1789 and still in print today. His home, The Wakes, is a museum with period furnishings where the original manuscript is on display. The gardens feature roses, herbs, vegetables, fruit and a topiary. Woodland and parkland are brought into his broad landscape design and provide pastoral views of the surrounding fields and forests. Directly across from The Wakes is the parish church of St. Mary. Stained glass windows in the church are particularly lovely. The St. Francis Window marks the bicentenary of White's birth with the saint preaching to species of birds featured in the naturalist's writings. His grave, marked only with his initials and death date, is in the northeast corner of the churchyard. Thatched-roof houses are scattered along quiet lanes. Following the ZigZag Path cut by White and his brother provides wonderful views of the village below.

The Mid Hants Railway, which runs between Alton and the town of Alresford (stations are signposted from the A31), steams its way through the countryside treating visitors to an excursion into a bygone era of transportation. The Watercress Line passes through Medstead/Four Marks, southern England's highest station, and Ropley, site of the locomotive yard. The stations have been restored in period style.

Alice Holt Woodland Park, about five miles northeast of Alton near Bentley, is a working forest famous for its wondrous oaks as well as its beautiful birds and butterflies. In modern times, Alice Holt Oak was used in the construction of the replica of Shakespeare's Globe Theatre in London. In past centuries, the forest supplied wood for the building of Britain's great naval fleets. There are well-identified hiking paths where explorers can enjoy the quiet forest and stunning wildlife. Visitors can rent bikes at the Forest Centre and picnic in the grounds.

Tichborne *(See Chapter 14)*

Chapter Thirteen

Hambledon

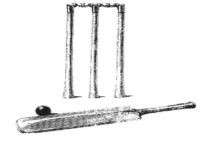

And
the Games Begin

There are several unique sports that have strong associations with England and British tradition, even though the games themselves may have originated in other parts of the world. Passed down through the generations, the activities generally evolved from simple forms of recreation using whatever "equipment" was at hand. From hurling a stone to picking up a stick and whacking it back, early athletes used their prowess to toss objects harder, hit them farther and generally best the other participants in any way they could. The rules sometimes changed from game to game and certainly from place to place—in the case of tennis, from monastery to monastery.

As early as the twelfth century, French monks were known to use the cloisters of their religious houses as precursors of modern tennis courts. Engaging in a game called "jeu de paume," they used their hands in the early days before racquets became part of the game. French kings built elaborate indoor and outdoor courts, and England's palaces of Greenwich, St. James, Hampton Court and Whitehall were fitted out with courts for the enjoyment of Henry VIII and his noble subjects.

Revolutions and rebellions consigned the sport to temporary obscurity. When it emerged again in nineteenth-century England, it was quite a different game. Sphairistike—ball game in Greek—was invented by Major Walter Clopton Wingfield, a retired cavalry officer. His game combined elements of court tennis and badminton. Lawn tennis, as it came to be called, quickly gained popular recognition. A section of lawn at The All England Croquet Club was transformed into a tennis court, and the name of the club became The All England Croquet and Lawn Tennis Club. They held the first Wimbledon tennis tournament there in 1877.

Croquet, viewed as a genteel game for the leisure set, came to England from Ireland in the 1850s. The game may have its roots in contests staged by French peasants in the thirteenth century. These early gamesmen propelled balls through willow branch hoops. It is said that London's Pall Mall takes its name from "paille maille," a French ball and mallet game. When a full complement of equipment was marketed as a game set by a London sporting goods firm, croquet caught on and was adopted by both men and women as a fashionable pastime.

In 1868, Walter James Whitmore released a book on the particulars of the game. Within a few short years, national competitions followed and the attraction to croquet grew throughout the British Empire. However, with the rise of lawn tennis, the popularity of croquet began to fade. Through recent decades, it has seen a revival as a casual, backyard, warm-weather rivalry. On the other end of the spectrum, there are more than twenty countries worldwide that play competitive croquet today.

The object of the children's game battledore and shuttlecock was for players to bat a feathered cork back and forth as many times as possible without the cork touching the ground. It was played hundreds of years ago in Greece, China, Japan and India. The earliest participants joined in a collaborative effort to keep the shuttlecock airborne, but then the contest became more interesting when colleagues became competitors and faced each other across a net. British officers serving in India brought "poona," as the game was called there, back to England. It was introduced at an 1873 social gathering at the Duke of Beaufort's elegant country house—Badminton.

It didn't take long for badminton clubs to form, which elevated the relaxed game to a spirited sport. The first All England Championships were held in 1899, and the International Badminton Federation was formed in 1934. Badminton, played at a astonishingly fast pace, premiered as an Olympic sport in 1992 at the Barcelona games.

Lawn bowling most likely derived from a stone tossing game played by Roman soldiers. As they traveled through the empire, the variations of the game were taken up by the local populations. Italians had "bocce," the French played "boules" and the English bowled on the green. The game became so popular in England and on the Continent that it was banned when play interfered with more important concerns. Men were supposed to perfect their archery skills to defend king and country, rather than improve their bowling technique.

The balls used in the game are of various weights and have a flat spot so when they begin to slow down they roll toward the bias. The object is to earn points by skillfully judging the speed, using the curve and adeptly delivering the ball as near as possible to the white ball known as the jack. It is a deliberate exercise in concentration and consistent performance.

Above all, the classic English game is cricket. The traditional cricket bat is made of sleek willow with a cane handle. The hard ball is cork and string covered in red leather with white stitching. There are eleven players on each team, and the complex rules that govern the game are hard to grasp.

Bowler, batsman, pitch, and stumps are foreign words to the uninitiated. A batsman guards the stumps (three thirty-two inch high uprights positioned in the ground behind the batsman) at one end of the pitch. Another batsman is stationed at a second set of stumps at the opposite end of the pitch. The bowler rotates his arm above his head in a smooth motion, deftly controlling the speed and spin of the ball, and sends it down the pitch toward the batsman. He is attempting to knock over two horizontal crosspieces (bails) resting on the stumps, and the batsman is trying to prevent that from happening by hitting or deflecting the ball into the field. When the ball is hit into the field, each batsman runs to the opposite wicket. Runs are scored by the batsman who hit the ball, generally by running from one wicket to the other—sometimes more than once— or by striking the ball and sending it into or over the boundary fence (in which case, they do not need to run as they score automatically). A batsman is out if the bails are knocked off the stumps by the bowler, if the bails are knocked off when the batsmen are running between their wickets, or the ball is hit and then caught by a fielder. Various team activities precipitate a change of bowlers and batsmen through the course of the innings. After a long afternoon of play, a match often ends in a draw.

Cricket-playing nations compete in a series of Test Matches which are scheduled throughout the summer. The first English cricket team competed in Australia in 1861. The County Cricket Championships date from 1873.

Manuscripts from the Middle Ages show illustrations of a game that resembles cricket. It was played at fairs and during festival celebrations and across rural England in the centuries that followed. The Hampshire village of Hambledon made significant contributions to the evolution of the modern version of the sport. For today's spectators, taking in a cricket match provides the opportunity to set out the picnic hamper, pop the cork on a bottle of champagne and watch the white-clad players do their best to win the day.

Hambledon Today

Broadhalfpenny Down stands deserted in the quiet of the early evening. It's not difficult to reach back into the past and picture the men of Hambledon shedding their black velvet-collared blue jackets and taking up their positions on the field. This is the "cradle of cricket." A stone obelisk near the fence pays tribute to the grounds of the famous Hambledon Cricket Club, 1750–1787. Etched in stone is a ball with two bats resting against either side of a wicket. The pavilion on the far side of the down is new and attests to the ongoing commitment to the sport in modern times. Since the late 1950s, The Broadhalfpenny Brigands Cricket Club has supported competitive play and makes certain that cricket matches continue to be played in this historic setting. Today, the Hambledon Cricket Club play their matches at Ridge Meadow, not far from the village.

Just across the road is the Bat & Ball. The public house served as the clubhouse for the Hambledon cricketers and is filled with memorabilia regaling the heyday of the game. The bar is the heart of the house. Comfortable leather chairs face the fireplace over which hangs a gleaming cricket bat. In the early days, the particulars of village matches were agreed to in the pub and lively conversations about the game still take place beneath the photos that venerate the village players' considerable contributions to the sport.

Hambledon village is a few miles from this illustrious corner of cricket history. High Street, where once there was a private school, a pub, tea room, shops and a saddlery, is lined with private homes, many from the seventeenth century or earlier. Several of the houses in the village date from this time but have Georgian fronts. The Church of St. Peter and St. Paul has a thirteenth-century exterior with a tranquil interior that spans the centuries: Saxon features alongside a new chapel honoring the recent millennium. The colors of the Hambledon Volunteers who fought against Napoleon proudly decorate the church. A yew tree in the churchyard is almost a thousand years old. It seems to guard the gravestones, many of which memorialize notable cricket players.

The rustic stable yard at George House appears much as it did in the eighteenth century when the coaching house was the site of daily departures that met up with the Portsmouth to London stagecoaches at nearby Petersfield. The Vine, in West Street, is a free house pub and restaurant dating from the sixteenth century.

There are relaxing walks through and around the village past pleasant cottages and out onto the downs. The rolling countryside around the village begs to be explored. Speltham Down teems with wildflowers. Cowslips make way for daisies and varieties of orchids color the chalk downs with breathtaking beauty.

Finding Your Way

Hambledon is approximately ten miles north of Portsmouth. Take the A3 north to the B2150 at Waterlooville. Follow the B2150 about four miles northwest in the direction of Denmead. The village is signposted.

Nearby Places of Interest

Portsmouth, about ten miles south of Hambledon, is the naval hub of England. Flagship Portsmouth, located at the Portsmouth Naval Base dockyard, offers the opportunity to board the completely restored HMS Victory and learn about Lord Nelson's ship and the 1805 Battle of Trafalgar. The Tudor navy's flagship, Mary Rose, can also be seen. Both vessels and others are on display with the modern warships near the Royal Naval Museum, which houses an extensive collection of exhibits tracing Britain's maritime history. The D-Day Museum at Southsea recalls the events of June 6, 1944 when British, Canadian and American military forces landed in Normandy. The Overlord Embroidery, made by twenty women from the Royal School of Needlework, details the history of the invasion in a massive tapestry that has thirty-four eight-foot by three-foot panels. Photographic displays and scenes feature objects from the period. An impressive audio-visual presentation tells the story with original footage and archival film.

ॐ   ॐ   ॐ

Butser Ancient Farm, about seven miles northeast of Hambledon, is a look at life in the Iron Age of Britain, about 300 B.C. The re-created Celtic settlement functions as an outdoor laboratory for archaeological study. Visitors can see rare breeds of cattle, sheep and goats, as well as housing, fields and crops. Interactive activities include grinding corn, feeding livestock, crafting clay pots and lending a hand to the spinning. It is the site of Europe's largest crop trial program.

Tichborne *(See Chapter 14)*

Chapter Fourteen

Tichborne

The

Tichborne Dole

The thin light of day was fading as heavy mist seemed to swallow up the stones of the old manor house. Indoors, a maid lit the candle near Lady Mabella's bed. The good woman was dying.

Her husband, Sir Roger Tichborne, an arrogant, rough man, had little time for Mabella and less consideration for the peasants who worked on his vast estates. His family had owned the land since Saxon times, and he was fiercely dedicated to preserving his heritage, expanding his holdings, and remaining in the good graces of Henry II.

Mabella realized her time was growing short. She begged Sir Roger to set aside something in her memory for the less fortunate of the parish. Her simple request was that each year on Lady Day a dole of bread for the poor should be distributed.

Cruelly, he responded with a challenge—one he never imagined she could meet. Roger directed that she should get up from her bed and follow him out into the night. If Mabella could carry a lighted torch around one of the fields, he would set aside as much land as she could cover before the firelight went out and allow the crop grown there to be made into bread for the poor.

It took all her energy to stand. A maid helped her into a dress made of coarse fabric and fastened a warm cloak around her shoulders. Her servants carried her across the yard to the edge of the field. Others gathered in small groups, curious about what was taking place, knowing their lady was too ill to leave her bedchamber and not understanding why she was out in the damp, evening air.

The torch was lit and Lady Mabella took a few steps, sinking down into the freshly turned soil. On her knees, torch in hand, she dragged herself forward between the furrows. The earth dampened her skirt. The weighty wool trailed through standing water and slowed her progress.

Mabella struggled on as the torchlight flickered. Miraculously, she managed to crawl around a plot encompassing twenty-three acres of rich, fertile, Tichborne land before the flame sputtered out.

Fearing her husband would not honor his promise, the dying woman cursed any Tichborne successor who did not faithfully continue the annual charitable act of feeding the poor. She warned that if the dole was stopped, the family name would die. She compounded the denunciation by declaring that the house would tumble down, the male line would not prosper, and seven daughters would follow.

Each year after Lady Mabella's death, loaves of bread were handed out to all who came to Tichborne House on March 25, Lady Day, which commemorates the Annunciation of the Blessed Virgin Mary. This practice was a highlight of the village year for six centuries until 1796 when applicants became so unruly and destructive that the charitable event was abandoned.

Seven years later, in 1803, Lady Mabella's fateful words echoed hauntingly when a wing of the house collapsed. During these years, Sir Henry Tichborne fathered child after child—seven daughters, but no son.

One of Sir Henry's younger brothers, Edward, changed his name to Doughty and his wife gave birth to a son, but the boy died at an early age. Mindful of the old curse and in hopes of removing obstacles to perpetuating the male line, Sir Henry immediately revived the dole. The family name survived through James, another of Sir Henry's brothers, when his son, the long awaited heir, was born.

Loaves of bread were no longer distributed after the charitable giving was restored. Instead, flour ground from wheat harvested from Lady Mabella's field was scooped from a bin and given to the villagers from Tichborne and nearby Cheriton as they gathered on the front steps of Tichborne House. Even when flour was rationed during and immediately following World War II, coupons were donated to make certain the ancient Tichborne Dole continued to be administered.

The annual Dole Day celebration still begins by blessing the flour and offering a traditional prayer for the soul of the benefactress. Members of the family personally measure out a portion for each adult and a half-portion for every child. Through the centuries, to this day, Lady Mabella's field is still known as "The Crawls."

Tichborne Today

Ticceburn, as the village was named in written records dating from the tenth century, was a great estate held by the Bishop of Winchester. Saxon farmers tilled the land and paid their rents to the bishop. Sweet ale, clear ale, loaves, cheese, pigs, sheep and oxen were the currency the farmers used to satisfy the landlord. Around 1135, the estate was divided, and the bishop granted manor lands to Walter de Tichborne. The Home Farm, Grange Farm, and Tichborne Park are still owned by the family.

The village church of St. Andrew stands high on a hill overlooking the watercolor scene of Tichborne's tranquil farms and emerald fields. In the churchyard, headstones tilt toward one another as the breeze rustles through the long grass.

The original church dates from the mid-eleventh century. Later, the southern and then the northern aisle were added to enlarge the existing structure. The small window on the east wall was replaced with a large tracery window in about 1330.

There are several monuments to the Tichborne family, the most splendid of which is the vividly painted tomb erected in 1621 to honor Sir Benjamin and his wife Lady Amphillis. The figures on the base of the tomb represent their seven children.

During the Reformation, the family held tenaciously to their Catholic faith. In 1603, Sir Benjamin pledged his loyalty to James I and, as sheriff, assisted in delivering Hampshire's much needed support to the new king. Though St. Andrew's is an Anglican church, the north aisle, where Sir Benjamin's impressive tomb is located, is used as a chapel for Catholic services.

Another notable monument commemorates the death of Sir Richard Tichborne's young son in 1619. A gypsy curse foretold that on a specific day, the boy would drown. Legend says servants took the child to Gander Down, far away from the river. Ironically, he fell from his carriage and drowned in a water-filled rut made by the wheel of a cart.

The church also has remnants of a medieval painting of St. Christopher on the north wall. Following the Reformation, the original rendering was covered over with whitewash, which was often done to nullify the practice of decorating churches with works of art commemorating Catholic saints.

Down the hill, through an arch of ancient trees, Tichborne House and Park lie nestled in the Itchen valley. Records show that in 1293 permission was granted to hold religious services at Tichborne House, and not long after, a private chapel was constructed there. The present structure dates from 1803 and is still the home of Tichborne descendents. The raised porch of the house has large, Italianate columns. It is on these steps that the family gathers to hand out the Dole flour every March 25.

Today, The Old School House, Church Cottage, Itchen Cottage, Garden Cottage, The Old Post Office as well as centuries-old farmhouses are private residences that line the quiet roads and fields near the manor house. Across the road from Tichborne Park is The Crawls—the twenty-three acres of open field that serves as a living legacy to Lady Mabella and her contribution to the life and times of Tichborne.

Finding Your Way

Tichborne is located about five miles east of Winchester. Follow the A31 in the direction of New Alresford. Turn south onto the B3046. Drive approximately one mile, turn west onto a country lane and follow the sign to Tichborne.

Nearby Places of Interest

Winchester, approximately five miles west of Tichborne, is Roman in origin and one of England's loveliest small cities. After the Norman invasion, it served as William the Conqueror's capital. Domesday Book, the massive inventory of English landholdings, was compiled here. Winchester Cathedral was consecrated in 1093. Today's gothic church dates primarily from the fourteenth century, but wonderful examples of Norman architecture remain. The window memorializing Jane Austen is in the north aisle. Scholars attend classes in Winchester College's fourteenth-century buildings. The City Museum, near the cathedral, features Victorian-era shop fronts as well as remnants of the Celts, Romans and Saxons who once occupied the surrounding countryside.

New Alresford (pronounced Allsford), about two miles north of Tichborne, is a market town offering a wide main street lined with stores, antique shops, fine arts galleries and restaurants. A riverside walk passes the site of the old fulling mill in operation during the thirteenth century when the area was a profitable wool center. Early in its history, devastating fires spread through the town, igniting the many thatched roofs. Most of the roofs are now of tile. The Swan Hotel on West Street served as a coaching stop on the busy London to Southampton route. Watercress farms are plentiful in the area.

Cheriton, a little over a mile south of Tichborne, whose residents share in the right to receive the Tichborne Dole, has a picturesque village green bordered by a few small shops and cottages. The Flower Pots Inn, an old pub, has its own on-site brewery.

Hinton Ampner Garden, located about three miles southwest of Tichborne, is an exquisite collection of formal and informal scented plantings administered by the National Trust. The twentieth-century shrub garden displays the creativity of designer Ralph Dutton, the last Lord Sherbourne. The house is open to view and features Italian paintings and fine English furnishings.

Chawton *(See Chapter 12)*
Hambledon *(See Chapter 13)*

Chapter Fifteen

Wherwell

The
Fine Art of Thatching

Eye-catching cottages wear their thatched roofs like broad-brimmed bonnets that shelter the walls below. They stand proudly along peaceful village lanes, on the edges of winding country roads, and deep in lush, leafy woodlands.

The shape and simplicity of the architecture contrast cleanly with its surroundings. White walls striped with wood, muted brickwork or well-weathered stones frame miniature windows evoking storybook memories. Smartly trimmed thatch, coloring to a dark chocolate, drapes over the ridge of a roof to form a luxuriously thick covering.

From the time when early Britons first felt the need for roofs over their heads, thatch has been used as a building material. Dwellings of wattle and daub—twigs, small branches, mud and straw—could only support something lightweight so it was practical to use whatever grass and straw could be found. As buildings became more substantial, roofs fashioned from longer-lasting products seemed more sensible. The beauty and charm of the thatched roof has never lost its attraction.

Through the years, homeowners have perpetuated its presence. Artists continue to capture its whimsical perfection in their paintings. Passersby admire the clever construction that floats between house and heaven.

The separate pieces of straw or reed are hollow so a thatched roof rests lightly on the rafters of an old cottage. The thatch material can be suitably shaped to fit the contours of a building with the careful trimming of pinnacles, gables and eaves providing visual interest. Sometimes the space below a window is worked in an attractive, ornamental apron. The overall effect is beautiful.

Thatching a roof is a labor-intensive undertaking that may take weeks to complete. The thatcher climbs up and down a ladder carrying tied bundles to the roof where he painstakingly puts down an under layer and pegs it to the roof beams. The upper layer follows, covering the first. Then the final layer is laid along the ridgeline.

The thatch along the ridge of the roof can be worked in many decorative finishes. The patterns are often distinctive to individual regions of the country. Some thatchers add a small variation to the design—their signature on a lofty masterpiece. And at one time they hid a tool or memento in the roof for the next thatcher to discover.

Some roofs are fitted with wire mesh to deter birds from pulling out the thatching material. When straw is used, the entire roof is often protected. If the roof is made of reeds, generally only the ridge, gables and eaves are covered.

Decorative corn dollies—usually pheasant-like creatures—perch on the tops of many roofs. The intent is to bring luck to the household.

These engaging pieces are made in various ways. Sometimes straw is enclosed in wire mesh and then the net is shaped into final form. Another method is to build the bird from wire to which straw is tied and then trimmed into head, wings and tailfeathers.

Thatchers begin as apprentices, and after years of perfecting their skills as journeymen, reach the status of master. They generally live in areas where they work—local men. In the past, the craft was passed from one generation to the next. Today, fathers still teach long-established techniques and personal artistry to their sons.

These able craftsmen have their own unique language. They talk about Long Straw, Combed Wheat Reed, Norfolk Reed and using Sedge, a water grass, for trim. Brow course, nibs and gadds are used in the same sentence as saddle and yealm. They recall the old days when heather was used in the north and describe how tall, thin stalks of lavender were a surprisingly strong and fragrant thatching material.

It's easy to put into words the effect these striking thatched works of art has on the observer: enchanting, delightful, impressive, magnificent. When travelers encounter one of these sparkling gems, they have one more wonderful memory of England to take away with them.

Wherwell Today

As the steep incline curves past the White Lion toward the Chilmark stone war memorial, the beguiling thatch-capped cottages of Wherwell come into view. White walls flash in the sun and the billowy outlines of their roofs stand out against the sky. Simple plaques identify a few: The Old Malt House, Aldings. There are stone walls with thatched tops and a breezy, island-like, thatched garden hut where tulips and small white blossoms merrily trim a stone terrace.

Using the church steeple as a compass point, the road passes over the fast-running River Test and turns toward the woods. Gleaming trout shoot through clear, cold water as it rumbles and rushes under the bridge. A fairy-tale cottage with bright blue windows holds its ground as the river splashes close to its wooden fence. Soft yellow washes the walls of another house. Its deep thatch sweeps down the side wall almost touching the low garden bushes.

St. Peter and Holy Cross Church stands at the wooded end of this quiet, cottage-dotted lane. The present church was rebuilt in the nineteenth century but has some Saxon and medieval sculptures from an earlier church. There is also a tomb thought to be that of a fourteenth-century abbess from Wherwell Abbey which once occupied the land that adjoins the old churchyard. In 1999, glass-engraved windows were installed in the south wall to mark the millennium. The artist captured symbols of the resurrection and easily recognized representations of Wherwell village life: lush, purple orchids that grow on the common, snowdrop blossoms that cover the churchyard in spring, village buildings, and famous local River Test trout. The weathered, wood-shingled bell tower looks down on the carved church porch, speckled gravestones and the menacing medieval double heads that guard a stone mausoleum almost hidden by the trees.

The Priory, a private residence, can be seen just over the churchyard wall. The graceful house gives no hint that an abbey founded by Queen Elfrida in the tenth century once stood on this site. Elfrida's abbey was destroyed during Henry VIII's Dissolution of the Monasteries. When modern drainage excavations were made under the river, what may be stones from the abbey—some decorated with scrollwork—were uncovered along with several artifacts.

The White Lion pub stands at the top of the main road. A cannonball from the Civil War is displayed in the bar, and a lovely garden beckons around back. In the old days, a trace horse was stabled here. Horse-drawn wagons heaped with wheat or barley often needed help to negotiate the steep hill. For a modest fee, the trace horse was tethered to the cart to provide additional "horsepower." When they reached the top, the horse was unhitched and trotted back down the hill on his own.

Lush water meadows stretch from the banks of the River Test. Local equestrians saunter down the road on horseback, touching riding crops to their hats in a friendly greeting.

Beds and borders show signs of avid gardening. This idyllic village is a living example of the preservation of an age-old art. It wears its thatch like a crown almost defying the passage of time.

Finding Your Way

Wherwell is approximately three miles south of Andover. Follow the A3057 to the B3420. The village is signposted.

Nearby Places of Interest

Whitchurch Silk Mill, about six miles northeast of Wherwell, occupies a small island on the River Test. It is a working museum where silk yarn is fashioned into fine fabric. Visitors can view Victorian machinery and traditional weaving techniques at the picturesque mill which has been in use since the 1820s.

Highclere Castle, about ten miles north of Andover, is the home of the Earls of Carnarvon. Their ancestors, the Herbert family, acquired Highclere in the late seventeenth century. The setting of the house is stunning as are the many rooms. Egyptian artifacts from the fifth earl's archaeological expeditions are on display at the castle. He sponsored the explorations of Howard Carter. In 1922, they revealed the burial place of Tutankhamun, the finest untouched tomb ever discovered in the history of Egyptology. A few months after the entrance to the tomb was uncovered, Lord Carnarvon died in Cairo. The gardens feature glasshouses in which fruit and vegetables for the main house were grown in Victorian times. Grapefruit, figs, grapes and oranges as well as bananas, rice and coffee thrive today. There is a Monk's Garden, a lavender walk and Secret Garden with serpentine paths.

The Museum of Army Flying, about five miles southwest of Wherwell, focuses on the history of aviation beginning in the 1880s with balloons, kites and airships through to the present day. Separate areas address the activities of the Royal Flying Corps from 1912–18, The Royal Artillery, military gliders from 1940–45, and the birth of the modern Army Air Corps. Aeronautically inclined visitors can enjoy a helicopter simulator and fascinating interactive science and education displays.

Mottisfont Abbey Garden, House and Estate, located approximately ten miles southwest of Wherwell, was an Augustinian priory before it became a private residence at the time of Henry VIII's Dissolution of the Monasteries. The house has been greatly transformed through the years and showcases The Whistler Room, a salon decorated with murals by Rex Whistler. The breathtaking gardens feature the National Collection of Old-Fashioned Roses where more than three hundred varieties can be seen. There are plane trees, Spanish chestnuts, beeches, cedars, climbing wisteria and a gothic summerhouse, among many other impressive horticultural attractions.

Tichborne *(See Chapter 14)*

Less Familiar Words and Terms

Almshouses—homes for the poor supported by charitable contributions

Chancel—section of a church nearest to the altar, occupied by the clergy and choir

Cloister—covered walkway in a monastery, usually arched, bordering a central, open, grassy area

Cotswold Lion—a descriptive name for the Cotswold breed of sheep referring to its large size and heavy fleece

Combe—sloping valley near the side of a hill

Cruck Timbers—curved timbers serving as support beams for the roof of a building

Dissolution of the Monasteries—disbanding and destruction of English religious houses during the reign of Henry VIII

Dole—a charitable allotment

Domesday Book—William the Conqueror's survey, dated 1086, detailing the value and inventory of landholdings in England

Ducking Stool—chair attached to a plank of wood in which a person, usually a woman, would be plunged under water as a punishment for gossiping or other offences

Hypocaust—Roman system where furnace-generated hot air flowed through spaces under the floor and in the walls to distribute heat

Kissing Gate—enclosure with gates arranged so people can move from one area to another in zigzag fashion, but animals are prevented from passing through

Knot Garden—intricate, geometric patterns made from hedges or shrubs clipped low to the ground outlining small beds filled with colored stones or plants

Lych-gate—entry gate to a churchyard sheltered by a roof, generally having a place to rest a body or coffin within the covered area

Manor—the manor house and surrounding land which might include one or several villages

National Trust—an organization established in 1894 to hold and maintain land and buildings in trust for the people

Parterre—a large garden with pathways between plant beds

Reformation—religious movement denying papal authority and establishing Protestant churches

Reredos—decorative carvings or paintings in back of a church altar

Rood Screen—divider made of stone or wood displaying a crucifix or rood, which separates the nave from the chancel in a church

Roof Bosses—artistically rendered carvings, often of heads, detailed scenes or intricate foliage, generally found in churches

Tithe Barn—structure built by a monastery or the lord of the manor to store tithes, one-tenth of the yield from the land paid to the priest or rector as an endowment

Tracery—ornamental, interlacing framework, as in a window

Wattle and Daub—twigs and branches covered with a mixture of mud and straw to form the walls of a cottage, hut or small structure

Weepers—figures on the base of a tomb often representing children of the deceased

Wolds—rolling, open countryside

Wool Churches—churches rebuilt or embellished by wealthy wool merchants

Woolpack—covering tied on each of four corners to protect wool during transit to market

About the Author

Marge D. Hansen grew up in Skokie, Illinois, a suburb of Chicago where she began her editing/writing career. Hansen has held editorial positions on publications across the country dedicated to technical as well as lifestyle, landscaping, interior design, parenting, food and travel subjects. She has edited fiction and non-fiction books, and as a freelance writer contributes to a variety of magazines and Web sites.

Having supervised the construction of several houses for her family, Hansen is captivated by artful design and has made this interest in architecture an important part of her travels. An avid reader, she is intrigued by stories and legends that provide a sense of place and offer insight into the people who infuse a scene with life.

European cities have always been among her favorite destinations, but it is the quiet villages and country lanes that Hansen prefers. She is a frequent visitor to England, but never could have predicted on her first visit almost three decades ago that her travels there would one day lead to writing a book about the pleasures of wandering its charming backroads and byways.

Hansen lives with her husband and favorite traveling companion, Richard, outside Denver, Colorado.

About Poncha Press

Poncha Press was founded in late 1999. The company strives to recognize new writing talent and to publish quality works of "first fiction" and non-fiction writing. Our mission is to identify unpublished and talented writers and make their work available to readers. The company intends to publish books in a wide range of genres.

Poncha Press donates a portion of its annual profits to U.S. charities that are dedicated to improving the welfare of animals. We are located in Morrison, Colorado, in the foothills of the Rocky Mountains. For more information about Poncha Press or our books, please visit our website at www.ponchapress.com.

Order Form

Fax Orders: (303) 697-2385. Send this form.
Telephone Orders: 1-888-350-1445.
Have your credit card available.
Internet Orders: www.ponchapress.com

Quantity	Title	Price
———	*An English Experience*	$17.95 (US)
———	—————————	———

Name: ———————————————————

Address: —————————————————

City: —————————— **State:** —— **Zip:** ———

Telephone: —————————————————

E-mail address: ————————————————

Please add 5.0% for products shipped to Colorado

Shipping
US - $4 for 1st book & $2 for each additional book
International - $9.00 for 1st book & $5 for each additional

Circle One: Visa   MasterCard   AMEX   Discover

Card Number: ————————————————

Name on card: —————————— **Exp. date:** —— / ——

X